NOTHING
QUITE LIKE IT

An American-Irish Childhood

By the same author

The Politics of Irish Drama
Shakespeare's Serial History Plays
Yeat's Poetic Codes

NOTHING QUITE LIKE IT

An American-Irish Childhood

Nicholas Grene

SOMERVILLE PRESS

Somerville Press,
Dromore, Bantry,
Co. Cork, Ireland

First published 2011

Designed by Jane Stark
seamistgraphics@gmail.com
Typeset in Adobe Caslon

ISBN: 978 0 9562231 59

Printed and bound by GraphyCems,
Villatuerta, Navarra, Spain

To the memory of

David Grene (1913–2002)

and

Marjorie Glicksman Grene (1910–2009)

'Mud, mud, glorious mud
Nothing quite like it for cooling the blood.'

Michael Flanders and Donald Swann,
'The Hippopotamus'

In the henhouse, Clash farmyard

Prologue

Mine was not a miserable childhood, though it was not idyllically happy either. I did not have to struggle with the deprivations of poverty, the hardships of oppression and discrimination; nor did I trip thoughtlessly through the fields to school. All that defines my childhood as distinctive is that it was odd. I grew up in that smallest of minorities, an Irish Protestant rural community, but I wasn't even of that community. To be Protestant in Ireland in the 1950s was not to be Catholic. Well I wasn't that; but I wasn't properly Protestant either. When I reached a stage of adolescence at which it seemed an occasion for boasting, I used to boast that I was an Anglo-Irish, American, Polish Jew. There weren't a whole lot of us belonging to that particular sub-group attending Ballinatone National School, Ballinaclash, Rathdrum, Co. Wicklow from 1952 to 1957. Just me, out of the total school enrolment of thirteen.

And it didn't help that my father was a 'professor'. Just what a professor was or did may have been quite vague in some people's minds. Especially when it took the form of professing classics in the University of Chicago through the autumn and winter months, while farming in Wicklow in the spring and summer. Out hunting, my father used to be saluted by the huntsman as 'Commander': Captain, Major, Commander, Professor—such were the assortment of more or less interchangeable honorifics sported by people who hunted for sport. Still, to have a father who was a professor promoted an uncomfortable sense within schools that my sister and I had an obligation to be clever. Just what they would have thought if they had realized our mother was a class of a professor too—or had been—and took time out from preparing potatoes for the men's dinner to write books on Heidegger or translate treatises on African anthropology from German doesn't bear thinking about. That, at least, we were spared.

What this memoir has to offer is the unusualness of my family and social situation, and the displaced viewpoint it gave me of what I experienced. When people ask where I live, I tell them confidently that I live in Clash and have done so for almost sixty years. Yet there is always in that declaration a tremor of untruth. It is not only that I have spent considerable time in those sixty years away from Clash— in boarding-school, at college, working in Britain, on study leave in France or America. It is the rootedness, the belonging, which seems to go with the claim to have lived in the one small village for such a length of time—that does not seem really mine.

CHAPTER ONE

Prehistory

My parents at about the time of their marriage in 1938

Asplash of brown on the left—could it have been a heap of sticks cut for winter?—a sharp right-hand turn across a hump-backed stone bridge, and we're there.

There must have been pre-five-year-old memories before this first moment of arrival in Clash, but I cannot swear to them. They may be just those digitally remastered re-recordings based on other older people's prompts.

I think I can remember landing on the quay at Cobh and being met by my father, who had gone to Ireland ahead of us to find and buy a farm. He packed us into a square black Ford Prefect with a wonderful indicator, a diminutive orange fin that flipped magically out of the car's black side when we were about to turn a corner. And to reach that quay I think I can remember having to take a little boat from the huge floating hotel that was the *Mauritania*.

The *Mauritania* continued to live with me for many years afterwards in the half of a cabin trunk plastered over with ss MAURITANIA labels that stood on end in my bedroom and provided my clothes with a hanging wardrobe. That kept nurtured in me the few fragments of shipboard life I could recall.

I was lost on the ship, though I didn't know I was lost. Somehow I had got left behind in the darkness of the ship's cinema. I have the distinct impression that I stayed on wilfully, having been told that the next part of the programme was too old for me. I even imagine that the unsuitably grown-up subject was a woman having a baby, but maybe it is only later Irish repressions, in which this would have been high on the list of unsuitable subjects, that makes me back-project the idea. Anyway, whatever the forbidden images that held me arrested to the screen when my older sister and whoever else had left, red alerts had gone out all over the ship to search for me before I was rediscovered happily absorbed by the first moving pictures that had ever come my way. The other *Mauritania* moment is anecdotal history, not owned by me as memory at all. Seated in the ship's dining-room, with full dinner-settings before us—let me make it the Captain's table to heighten the horror—I am reputed to have lifted up the beautifully cocked linen table-napkin and enunciated in my most carrying Midwestern voice: 'Mommy, what's this for?'

I have no recollection of what our farmhouse on Derby Road, near Lemont, Illinois looked like or felt like, but the airs and graces of linen napkins it is safe to assume it was without. Some photographs, the first in the family albums with colour, help me to piece together images that remain quite exotic to me. The round tower-like silo— what a silo was for, what you put into it, and how you got its contents out again are a mystery to me to this day; my father in peaked cap

My father watering the horse on the farm in Lemont, Illinois

gazing out over flat distances immensely wider than anything in our Wicklow hills; snow and more snow. Picturesque details added by my mother in her recollections of Lemont only make it more unreal: like the farmyard manure piled around the sides of the house to keep the pipes from freezing in the winter. Or there were the extremities of the heat in summer. 'There were just two possibilities', she always said. 'You could lie awake at night with the heat, happy at least in the thought your corn was growing, or you could sleep in the cool and wake up knowing it wasn't.'

I imagine having been out in the fields with my mother sowing that same Indian corn, when there was some crisis with the horse's harness, but what happened then is lost. My clearest recollections are of accidents and injuries to myself. I was chasing a straying guinea-fowl, with goodness knows what hope of catching it, and, climbing over a fence, I snagged my balls on the barbed-wire. The graze was taken very seriously—the wire might been rusty or contaminated with germs—and I had to have a tetanus shot. Tetanus and testicles are for ever connected in my mind.

My other American wound is still written on my body as a memory-prompt. On the palm of my left hand, at the base of the little finger, is a neat white scar some half an inch long. I walk into the toolshed; a sickle propped against the wall falls over and its tip cuts open my hand. That I remember, and even more the laundryman who happened by at the time and congratulated my mother on how brave I was. He must have come after the screaming had died down a little.

Beyond that it is all reconstruction, nothing of my own. I know as a matter of historical record that we visited Dublin in 1950 and spent several months at the home of my father's parents in Belmont Avenue, Donnybrook. My sister Rufus, four years older than me, remembers with disgust what a fuss was made of me as a male grandchild, and the fussing must have included the celebration of my third birthday. But of my paternal grandparents I can remember nothing; they were both to die before we returned to Ireland two years later. It always seemed odd to see the photographs of them from the one time they did visit the farm in America, looking strangely out of place in that sweltering Midwestern sun. And there am I, aged—what two?—in my playpen with my grinning red-haired sister standing beside me.

It is hard to conceive of your parents' lives before you were conceived, still less the time when they had wholly separate lives before they (so inevitably) met. But there is always the family folklore. In the case of my father, it was the spectacular success story of his student career at Trinity, vouched for by news-cuttings lovingly pasted into an album by his devoted and admiring parents. The profusion of strange-named entrance awards—exhibitions, sizarships and the like—he had won. Sizarship, it turned out, was the important one, providing support for students from poorer backgrounds. And then a Foundation Scholarship awarded in his first year when he was hardly eighteen. Most ordinary human beings took the Scholarship examination in their second year or later, but David Grene spent the six months after entering Trinity reading so much Latin and Greek that the unseen translations on his exam papers could not have been unseen to him. So it went on: appointed a lecturer while still an undergraduate, a double first of Firsts—whatever that was—in Classics and Ancient History; and the most tangible proof of it all, the large gold medal still in its red leather case that we could take out from the drawer in the table in the Clash sitting-room and finger with awe. You might be so clever you could be given a gold medal for it.

My father was one of those people whose destiny declared itself early, and declared itself as a double destiny. 'By the age of fifteen', he told me once, 'I knew there were two things I wanted to do in the world: read Greek and farm.' The Greek had begun much earlier than age fifteen at St Stephen's Green and then St Andrew's schools in Dublin, with inspiration coming from a splendidly talented teacher who would die dramatically for the benefit of the class in the role of Euripides' heroine Alcestis. The farming was less to be expected for a middle-class boy from Donnybrook in the 1920s with a father who worked as a book-keeper in the Sun Alliance Insurance Company. But there were distant cousins down in Tipperary, their cousinship made plain in spite of the distance by the shared surname with its odd spelling: they lived in Grene Park. To Grene Park, or to another nearby Grene residence close to Dundrum, Co. Tipperary, went my Dublin grandparents as paying guests for their annual holidays.

My grandfather, though a keen gardener, had no special interest in farming. (A photograph of him with a pitchfork at his shoulder misled me for years: strictly a holiday prop, I was eventually told.) But for my father, aged fifteen, there was a life-changing summer when the herd at Grene Park was out sick. Nicholas Grene, the Catholic Tipp. farmer for whom I am named, asked his young cousin David would he take on herding duty. He did, that summer and the following summer, and so the other twin passion of his life was in place. Somehow, however he managed it, he would find the

Grandparents John and Rose Grene with David (holding small girl on his lap) at Grene Park, Co. Tipperary; small boy on right is David's younger brother Jack

means to study Greek and to farm. Somehow, he succeeded. The son of the insurance company accountant, the grandson of the Royal Irish Constabulary Detective Inspector, was to become a Professor of Classics and part-time small farmer.

My mother's was just as striking a success story intellectually and academically, but that was never the way it was told. A PhD? Sure, she had a PhD: you needed a PhD just to sweep the streets in America. And her doctorate was from Radcliffe, not Harvard. That was one of the few things that really rankled with her: that as a woman in the 1930s you couldn't be awarded a Harvard doctorate. To my sister and me, of course, Harvard, Radcliffe, Wellesley (where our mother had been an undergraduate) were as mysterious as exhibitions and sizarships, the meaninglessly significant terms that landmarked our parents' lives at college. My mother was a philosopher. Why? According to herself, because she should have been a scientist (she majored in Zoology) but broke too many test-tubes in the lab. It had been a lonely childhood as an only child whose mother died when she was just thirteen. 'Is your mommy in?' said a salesman who came to the door. 'No, she's dead', said Marjorie.

Her father was a university professor of English in Madison, Wisconsin, a gentle unambitious man whom I met a couple of times when I visited America as a student. He had failed as a lawyer—hadn't the nerve to plead in court, according to his brutally honest daughter—and was encouraged by his wife to go back to graduate school at Yale and take a PhD in English. Appointed to a first post in the University of Wisconsin, he stayed there for the rest of his life, and it was in an old people's home in Madison that I last saw him. My mother's loneliness was compounded by her father going into a long period of withdrawn depression after his wife's death. When he did remarry, it was no better; my mother and her stepmother did not get on. So for Marjorie it was off to the east coast to college and eventually to Germany.

Germany was the one part of her early life about which my mother spoke with pleasure and animation. Two years there from 1931 to 1933, in Heidelberg and Freiburg, had obviously been of real importance. She had studied with Martin Heidegger and was to write one of the first books in English on his philosophy; yet apparently she was not a favourite student of his. There were three categories of people he didn't like: Americans, women and Jews. Three strikes and out for my mother.

Nineteen thirty-three was not the best year to be an American Jew studying in Germany. Already my mother's efforts to learn to cycle had come to a politically ill-omened end when her bike had run out of her control on a downhill slope and she had crashed into the editorial office of the Nazi party newspaper. With the accession of Hitler to power came the forms to be filled in with the crucial question: 'Were any of your ancestors Jewish?' '*Alles*', wrote my mother proudly, 'all of them', and left Germany.

The, to a Wicklow country-bred child, unimaginably romantic story of her grandfather's emigration to the United States in the 1860s was to her banal, uninteresting, paralleled as it was by the story

The young Marjorie in her study

of every family growing up in the Jewish middle-class community of Milwaukee where she was born. Her great-grandfather had been a 'gelehrte Herr' in a Polish ghetto, supported by his neighbours to allow him to study the Talmud. Her grandfather had run away to escape being drafted into the Russian army, had made it to Hamburg, had all his money stolen and was forced to work for years on the docks to re-earn his passage to America. He and a Jewish partner made their way across the continent from New York as pedlars, until they arrived at Chippewa Falls, then just a logging camp in Wisconsin. Under threat of being run out of town—'We don't want no dirty Jews here'—they were unexpectedly saved by being members of the Oddfellows, a friendly society like the Masons. A fellow-Oddfellow spoke up for them and they were allowed to remain, to live on, in the case of my great-grandfather, to become mayor and build the first brick house in Chippewa Falls.

From Milwaulkee, from Donnybrook, came my parents via Chicago to bring me to Ballinaclash, Co. Wicklow in September 1952.

The bridge over the river Avonbeg at Clash

CHAPTER TWO

The House

The farmhouse in Clash, taken from the bridge

The two perfectly symmetrical rooms downstairs, each a square 15 by 15 feet, the entrance hall between coming in right off the road, with its narrow wooden staircase going up the thirteen steps round the crooked corner that made it so hard to get furniture upstairs. Above, the two equally symmetrical main bedrooms and, squashed in the centre above the hall, the tiny bedroom that was mine. I always had a room of my own, all my life until I came to share one with my wife.

Not so our predecessors in the house. The Kirwans had had thirteen children, though probably not all of them at one time in Clash. They were mostly grown up by the time we arrived in 1952 and had only lived there for some five years, having bought the farm from another short-term owner, John Sheehan. You had to go back to the last tenant but two to reach the long-term occupant, Willie Woodbyrne, recalled by local residents with all the veneration due to the old and deep-rooted.

The Kirwans were a displaced Tipperary family, and were not really farmers but publicans by trade and temperament. They were all to go back to pub-owning: old Tom Kirwan to a pub in the cattle market area of Dublin, to be visited when my father went up to buy cows. Years later, the son, Matty, was to reappear in my life as the owner of the Lincoln Inn pub in Dublin and the Coliemore Hotel in Dalkey. In 1952 there were at least two of the younger children still at home in Clash. And it continued to be their home for a period of some two weeks of cohabitation after we arrived. Where did we all sleep? How did we squash in? I have no idea.

Of course the house wasn't just those two downstairs rooms, those bedrooms upstairs. At the end of the narrow entrance hall, with its irregularly curved stone wall, you walked through a door into the kitchen—the kitchen with its startlingly, unnecessarily high ceiling, with its great gape of an open fireplace occupying the full width, some quarter of the space, of the entire room. How did it come to take the form it did, added on at a right angle to the front block of the house, its door misaligned with the door coming into the original hallway? There was the wooden framework over on the left-hand side adjoining the fireplace, seemingly built to house a settle-bed. When the table was moved back from the bare concrete floor to receive its weekly covering of red Cardinal polish—that was one of the signature smells of my childhood—you could see the line of a wall that had run across the kitchen dividing it in two unequal parts. But had it ever been lofted, all of it or some of it? Could it have had some special use, for hanging sides of bacon, say, smoked in that inordinately large fireplace?

All this was to be the grown-up small change of conversation with visitors down the years as we ruminated on the oddity and antiquity of the kitchen—the house, we were told, had been burnt in the 1798 Rebellion. For now, in 1952, the kitchen was where you could be warm: at least you could if you were right up by the fire. There I can remember being bathed in a galvanized bath, surrounded by family and Kirwans. Every Lawrentian scene of the burly blackened Nottinghamshire miner stripped to his white skin, his back scrubbed down by his silent wife, I reimagine as a small boy in a tin tub by the wood fire in Clash.

There wasn't yet a bathroom. Well, there was and there wasn't. Two steep steps down from the kitchen out a door on the left was another added lean-to space, this one added within living memory. It was a part of the house, but was long-leased to the dispensary doctor. (I can see him still, his palsied hand shaking, as I stood rigid waiting for the needle with the diphtheria injection to go into my arm.) Here he examined his patients, and here was the only indoor toilet on the premises. To this toilet the Kirwans did not have access; it was never clear to me whether the doctor alone was allowed to perform his natural functions in the windowless concrete cubicle that stood between the two tiny rooms, or if patients were dispatched there to provide urine samples. In any case, until such time as the dispensary could be moved elsewhere—it went eventually across the bridge to a little hut-like building on the edge of the road at the other side of the village—we too were disbarred from the indoor lavatory.

Instead, there was the ingeniously constructed outside water closet. It was outside the house and it was a real water closet. Out you went from the kitchen through a door on the right into the sunken lower yard with its spout of water flowing in at one corner and flowing along the edge of the yard. Up three huge concrete steps to a little outhouse that was perched on the left, dwarfed between the gable chimney end of the kitchen and the lofted barn that abutted it. This outhouse was separated into two tiny dark divisions: the top side, with its own door, was the coalhouse into which tall gunny-sacks of coal were carried once a month and emptied onto the residual mulch of slack and catshit. But on the lower side, private and discreet, was the WC: the letters were painted on the door.

Down another steep step you went into the darkness and then up on to the wooden throne in which a neat round hole had been cut.

You sat down, bottom exposed, and below you, many feet of cold air below you, flowed the water from the stream in the yard. It was into this continuously running water that you dropped whatever you had to discard. It was carried swiftly and splashily through a culvert under the road into the even quicker running river Avonbeg and thence down to the Eighteen Arches, the always named end point of the river at the bridge in Arklow where it met the sea. The phrase 'raw sewage' always carries for me a rawness, an immediacy, that it does not perhaps have for other people.

I remember the time in the house with the Kirwans happily enough. It was good to be in a crowded space with young people—to me of course old, grown-up people—who petted, bathed and teased me. I was especially annoyed by their singing to me the then popular 'Walking my baby back home'. Somehow I had got it into my head that I was the 'baby' in question, and it was a mocking attempt to relegate me to a long-outgrown infancy. And so they sang it to wind me up. But it was a game; they loved winding me up. I knew they did, and loved it too.

For my mother, though, it must have been a time of moon-landing strangeness. Admittedly she was an American professor of philosophy who had not lived among fellow professors in a well-appointed apartment in Chicago; she had endured the snows of the farm in Lemont, the ducklings in the house, the pipe-protecting manure round the walls. But, when my father had gone back to America, which he did almost immediately in September 1952 to return to his teaching in Chicago, to find herself in a small Wicklow village, she and her two children sharing a farmhouse with a still extensive family of Kirwans, what must it have been like?

She remembers the thrill of the Syngean tramp who came to the door and addressed her as 'lady of the house'. The sheer romance of it almost had her out the door to join him on the roads. The more practical aspects were less delightful. There *was* running water in the house, as distinct from the gush from the spout in the yard. Well there was sometimes. Closely questioned by my mother on the waterless tap in the kitchen that confronted her one morning, Matty Kirwan replied that 'it would run by and by, Mrs Grene'. And so it did—sometimes. The water was piped from a tank in the kitchen garden that lay beyond the haggard alongside the hayshed. The rising ground that sloped up to this tank, leaving the house partly hunkered below ground level into the bottom of a hill, gave a gravity feed fall to the piped water. Hardly enough, though. When there hadn't been much rain and the tank got low, or (contrariwise) when the autumn skies opened, bringing torrents of mud down on the kitchen garden tank, the flow from the kitchen taps slackened to a dribble, or belched black and stopped. For some reason it made it worse that all the pipes were made of lead. I can still recall the bright gleam of copper as Jimmy King the plumber fitted the new pipes that represented the first modernization of the house in Clash. Copper for lead—that was progress.

I have lived so long in this house now, it is hard to excavate it back, to recover the rooms and their 1952 look and feel and uses. I had never much cause to spend time in the room to the left of the entrance hall, which came to be tenanted in turn by all three of my daughters— my son always had a room elsewhere. I cannot even remember who or what occupied it originally. The bedrooms upstairs were relatively stable. My sister's room was at one end where, as a special treat, I was allowed in to listen to Radio Luxembourg's Top Twenty broadcast at the challenging time of 11 to 12 on a Sunday night. You had to be very committed to knowing what was Number 1 to stay awake to the midnight hour when it was played. At the other end were my parents with their twin double beds, my father apparently never finding enough room for two in one double bed. Occasionally I found myself in one of these beds, after they had got up, sleeping on in the huge expanse of sheets and blankets. One morning, it appears, I nearly slept on there for ever when a Calor paraffin heater, left alight to keep me warm, started to smoke and came close to asphyxiating me.

The sitting-room downstairs, to the right of the hall door, is more secure in the mind because it has continued in its original function. It always was and remains a multiple purpose room. We did sit in it, all of us together or one at a time. It was my father's study, when he was home in Clash and studying. There was a large table with a litter of papers on it and the drawer that contained the velvet-lined box with the gold medal. It had a narrow iron fireplace, much disliked by my parents, and one of the first things they did was to cover with a thick layer of black paint its gaudy ornamentation. I can remember this because of my discovery of how adhesive black paint is when touched ever so experimentally with a fingertip. Years later, when my wife Eleanor and I had the fireplace pulled out to make way for a large stone substitute, the original was taken away and left outside. Over time the paint began to blister and peel away to reveal, down the sides of the old fireplace, inset into the iron frame, a set of charming art nouveau tiles: blue tulips on a yellow ground. In 1952, art nouveau was regarded as an intolerable vulgarity; by the 1970s, recovered and reclaimed, the tiles became a talking-point as they sat under hot dishes on our dinner-table.

The sitting-room was at its most special when transformed for Christmas. The Christmas tree occupied its own space, always in front of the window looking out on to the road. For weeks before we would cut out little pieces of gummed coloured paper to make paper chains for the tree. The taste of the gum is in my mouth still, the despair at my clumsiness when my crooked chain links, inadequately licked, came unlinked. There were candles too, at first; then—wonderful innovation—winking electric lights. And above, fixed to the bendy top shoot of the tree, was the silver-paper-covered star.

Christmases were generic: I cannot remember any one in particular, certainly not the first one in 1952, and they have become overlaid by all the Christmases since with my own children playing what was then my part. I remember a hula-hoop Christmas, which must have been quite a bit later, for the amazing sight of the huge red hula-hoops resting unwrapped on top of the usual rich jumble of flamboyantly covered parcels. There was a ritual of calling out the names of donor and donee: For Rufus from Mummy and Daddy, For Nicky from Mummy and Daddy, For Rufus from Santa Claus, For Nicky from Santa Claus. Santa Claus was an exploded myth in our house practically from the start; my older sister lost no time in putting me straight on this piece of adult flummery. But *additional* presents, over and above the major presents from our parents, were labelled as coming from Santa Claus.

For many years America was for me the smell of American clothes. There were these immeasurably grand boxes with, when opened, shirts wrapped in tissue paper, shirts in bold colours of red or green or check, shirts of stiff flannel unlike anything obtainable in Rathdrum or even Wicklow town. And there was the smell, the newness and freshness of it, the odour of the 'store', a store being something enormous and American, no possible kin to our own drapery shops, dark, homely and crammed with clothes shelved in higgledy-piggledly disorder. The American clothes—so often unwearable because they were the wrong size, the wrong material or just too liable to the stares and jeers of the Clashers—came from friends of my parents in Chicago. They were sent out of niceness and generosity, with just the smallest hint of Marshall Plan aid to the little Grenes in faraway Ballygobackward Ireland, posted or transported back by my father when he flew the then 15-hour journey across the Atlantic to be with us at Christmas.

The sitting-room too became the home of the phone when at last, some three years after their first arrival, my parents succeeded in persuading the Department of Posts and Telegraphs to install one. It sat on the large paper-strewn table, solid and black, with its wind-up handle protruding from its side, the handle you wound to call the operator. We were on a party-line: one ring was for the operator—to be ignored; two rings were for the Rectory; and at that point you listened very carefully because if there was one ring more, it was for us. There were times when the handle could be wound and wound and nothing would happen. The operators who manned the switchboard were based in the post office in Rathdrum where, according to my exasperated mother, they engaged in knitting-contests, each of them determined not to drop a stitch or fall a row behind by answering the phone. Very occasionally, long-distance calls would come through from America for my parents. There was the famous time when my father was called to the phone from our top fields, a good fifteen minutes' walk away, while some otherwise unidentified Flo from California was kept holding the line.

We did eventually repossess the downstairs bathroom from the dispensary doctor. We even got a bath to put in it. This was achieved through the Kirwan connection. Sally Kirwan was married to a man who owned the Corner House pub in Rathdrum. In their yard they had a long old bath used for washing out Guinness bottles—for this was still the time when publicans bottled and corked their own porter, recycling the bottles when empty. It came to us dark-stained and streaked with long years of stout dregs. My mother set to and painted it with a special sort of paint that was supposed to be waterproof, designed to form a respectable coating, concealing the discreditable signs of its former pub life. Sadly, the paint did not live up to its promised impermeability. After a while it began to crack and peel, coming away like sunburned strips of skin from the sides of the bath. It was one of the great pleasures of bathing to luxuriate in that long deep trough of hot water, large enough to swim in for someone of my size, and pick off strips of the paintskin, flaying piece after piece until the mottled brown of the Guinness-soaked ground was exposed.

When not in the bath myself, I stood or sat on those precipitous steps down from the kitchen, and watched my father bathe. He always bathed in the morning, somewhere between 6 and 7, and would call me to come and talk to him while he washed. The talking was mostly one way, but the image of the hairy male body and the splash of the water formed my idea of the way, as an adult, you started the day.

My father was gone for most of the winter, sometimes only up until Christmas if he taught just a single term in Chicago, sometimes until March if he taught two. But the big excitement of the year was the long trek to Shannon Airport, stuffed in the back of the black Prefect, or whatever was its successor, because our ancient second-hand cars never lasted long. There were sometimes overnight stops, with our Grene cousins in Cashel or Grene Park, or once, an occasion of unimaginable grandeur, at Cruise's Hotel in Limerick: the Christmas lights of Limerick remain in my memory as some sort of archetype of winter glitter and gaiety. And then the interminable wait, the positive sickness of anticipation, amid the crowd of expectant people outside the doors of frosted glass that kept us apart from the mystery of customs and immigration. Finally he came through those doors, that stout figure in his American clothes, so familiar and so exotic at once, vivid with energy, vitality and joy at seeing us. Once he had with him the Irish-American widow of a lawyer friend who had recently died, black-clothed and tear-stained, and we were caught in the cross-currents of emotion. The mourning and commiseration that were her due tangled and tainted our rapturous delight at my father's homecoming.

Back in the car, driving the long miles through the middle of Ireland, the talk flowed on, washing over the heads of my sister and myself. From my mother's side there was news of the farm, the cows, the pigs, the men. From my father came the latest university gossip, studded with obscure, bizarre names at the spelling of which, the shape or origin one could only guess: Otto von Simson was the easiest of them. There was a mysterious woman called Eve, who only years later resolved himself into Yves Simon. The names poured out, Nef, Eliade, Shils—Shils always the enemy, the leader of the opposing faction. As drowsy and half-awake we made our way into County Carlow, Leighlinbridge and the Fighting Cocks mingled in the sleepy mind with these exotica. And eventually there would be Shillelagh, Tinahely, Aughrim and the Straight Mile, bringing us finally to Clash and the house still there beside the big tree.

CHAPTER THREE

Ballinatone

Ready for school

It was buttons that turned me into a Protestant.

I had been too young to go to school in America, unlike Rufus—then still Ruthie before her red hair got her the Latin-derived nickname. Rufus had been to the nuns of St Alphonsus and so my parents, assuming that a convent school in County Wicklow couldn't be all that different from one in Lemont, sent her to the Catholic girls' school in Rathdrum. She hated it, stayed only a year, and was dispatched to board in Drogheda Grammar School. At not quite five, I was put in the local Catholic National School. It was not a hundred yards from our house, just across the Clash bridge, a one-teacher school with some forty kids held down by the elderly and reputedly severe Miss Doyle. I never got a chance to find out for myself whether or not she lived up to the reputation of being as cross as a briar. I left before the end of my first day.

I had been kitted out in a new suit of corduroy, jacket and short pants. Needing to go to the—outside, waterless—toilet, I found the buttons on my trousers too stiff for me to open, or maybe it was to close them again when they had been opened. Maybe they weren't on my trousers but my jacket. All I know for certain is the fumble of the fingers trying to make the buttons go into holes that seemed too small to fit them. How I got back to the house I have forgotten; I cannot have done anything as dramatic as run out unbuttoned across the bridge. But the shame had been too much for me. I could not face again those forty faces who would have been jeeringly aware of my incompetence with buttons. And so I was sent instead to Ballinatone, the alternative Protestant National School.

Ballinatone National School had been established in 1837, built in grey stone to accompany the little grey stone church beside it, allegedly to provide a perpetual curacy for a younger son of the Guinness family. Its date was written up over the door, and it must in its time have been one of the first National Schools, the system of universal elementary education set up by the British in Ireland before there was any such system in Britain. It was a single schoolroom that seemed quite full with no more than its 1952 muster of thirteen pupils: I was the unlucky added one above the dozen.

The teacher was tiny Miss Fitzsimons—tiny only in retrospect, glimpsed by me once some years after I had moved on and gained

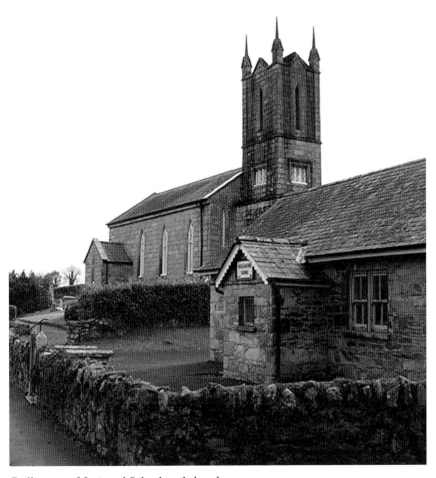

Ballinatone National School and church

nearly a foot in height above her. At the time I was conscious more of her glasses, the shreds of colour in her thin pale cheeks, and the chalk worked into the lines of her dry hands. Junior and Senior Infants, the First, Second, Third through to Sixth Classes had no more than one or two pupils in each. The room was heated by a Fireside paraffin heater with its glowing hemisphere of red surrounded by reflecting aluminium surfaces to scorch the shins of us Junior Infants. As you grew in age and experience, you were progressively banished backwards from the Fireside to the icy altitude of Sixth Class and the seriousness of the Primary Certificate.

For most of those in Ballinatone, this was to be the only schooling they were to have. The sons and daughters of small farmers or shopkeepers, they progressed up the school to age fourteen, the official school-leaving age. The girls did sometimes sit the Primary examination at that age; most of the lads, well before they were fourteen, had more or less stopped coming to school, had been driving tractors for years, were launched into an adult life of farmwork. No one that I can remember at Ballinatone went on to second-level, much less third-level education.

I arrived in my first week in Ballinatone clutching school primers of my sister's from St Alphonsus with their big block capitals: SEE, SEE, SEE. SEE SALLY RUN. Everything about them was clearly wrong. They had the wrong covers, the wrong thick blue bindings. The pictures of Sally and Peter were not like the pictures of John and Mary in the Irish books of Ballinatone. For a while I continued to bring them to class, ashamed though I was by their evident wrongness. And then, somehow or other, they got dropped in the pigpen, and the rich smell of pigshit provided a convincing reason for leaving them at home, and I could acquire my own copies of the John and Mary, Séan agus Nuala books that all the others had. My extremely strong Midwestern accent disappeared almost as quickly as the embarrassing American readers, and I tormented my parents by speaking in an exaggeratedly thick Wicklow country voice, doing my best to mimic my schoolmates.

Plasticene is my earliest memory of Ballinatone: the giving out of the lovely, clean, corrugated sheets of the different colours—yellow, blue, red, and the especially suggestive one called 'flesh'. Then, as you worked with them over the days, the colours got muddled, initially in candy-striped swirls until they ended up one indistinguishable mud brown. Tractors were the favourite thing to model. I never did acquire the skill of Norman Cassells or Howard Snell in shaping the big wheels in back, the tiny wheels in front, the oblong bulk of the body, the exhaust-pipe sticking erect up by the bonnet, much less the nuances of the moulded seat and steering-wheel. But then my horse-mad father had decided on a one-man resistance to modern technology and had determined to farm without a tractor. It wasn't until I was nineteen, going to a farm job to make holiday money in England, that I belatedly learned to drive a tractor.

Howard was older than me, and much taller, already nearing the end of his school-time. We cannot have overlapped in school for more than a year. I recall only a complicated swap transaction involving a toy lorry, a half a crown and a marmalade cat. I don't know now how it went but *we* ended up with the cat. Norman was my exact contemporary whom I greatly admired. Harry Brownrigg was younger and smaller than we were, shy with a stammer, as might well be expected from the youngest in a family of six with four bonny, apple-cheeked sisters ahead of him, all with the distinctively un-Catholic names of Irish Protestants at the time: Ruby, Beryl, Eunice (they were clearly running out of precious stones) and Alison.

To be not Catholic was to be Protestant; it was a uniform category of the other. Most of those at Ballinatone were Church of Ireland and attended the church behind the school on Sundays and high holidays. There were, though, 'Dippers' like the Brownriggs, marvelled at for their adult immersion baptism and their strict proscription of radio, TV, dances and other such frivolities. There were excited whispers that Harry's much older brother Austin had gone wild, defied his mother and taken to drinking, but nobody quite believed that. I, with a lapsed Protestant for a father, a non-religious Jew for a mother, was automatically counted as Protestant—and probably would have been such, even if it hadn't been for those troublesome buttons. I sat there and learned the kings of Israel and Judah with the best of them. (*All* the rulers of Israel were wicked, Ahab and Jezebel only the most notably wicked among them; an exceptional few of the kings of Judah were 'right in the sight of the Lord'.)

Three days a week—Mondays, Wednesdays and Fridays—the reading, writing and dictation were in Irish; the intermediate Tuesdays

and Thursdays were in English. In our lined copybooks we were taught
to form the big rounded letters of English, the separate, more angular
shapes of Irish. I very much admired the shape of the Irish 'a' but
found it very hard to write. I never could do very well at any sort of
handwriting and sank eventually into the squashed-up fist that shames
me to this day.

Irish was taught by the direct method, on the assumption that,
since it was our first national language, it was also our mother tongue.
That was not true for any of us, of course. Instead of acquiring
fluency by exposure to an Irish-language environment, we learned
to parrot whole phrases and sentences, not one word of which we
could distinguish or re-employ in another context. The hand shot
up: 'An bhfuil cead agam dul amach, más é do thoil é?' I can still
rattle it out (though probably not spell it correctly), and I knew it
was what you had to say when you wanted to go to the lavatory. But
goodness knows when I came to understand that I was saying 'Do I
have permission to go outside please?'

'Go outside' was not merely a euphemism. The lavatory was
indeed an outside toilet; Ballinatone, like Ballinaclash National
School, was without running water. At lunchtime, for those of us
who wanted to make ourselves cocoa, there was a visit to the nearby
Hewitt farmhouse where water could be boiled on the fire. It cannot
have been something that was done every day; I remember it dimly
as an exceptional event, being in the Hewitt kitchen, seeing the
cocoa powder mixed with a little milk, the steaming water poured
on to the chocolate paste, the beautifully iridescent bubbles on the
surface of the cocoa that was too hot to drink without blowing. Even
more rarely, once in the year, there was the much longer journey up
the same Greenan road to visit old Mrs Fitzsimons. Our teacher's
father had been steward in Ballinacor, the 1,500-acre wooded estate
that had belonged to the Kemmis family for generations since the
eighteenth century. We visited the big house annually for a Christmas
party the Kemmises gave for the schoolchildren. I can remember of

these occasions nothing but the stag's head with its thirteen-pointed antlers in the huge entrance hall.

Mrs Fitzsimons lived on with her other daughter Bessie—our teacher's name, which none of us knew at the time, was Maud—in the steward's house in the depths of the Ballinacor woods. It was inconceivable that anyone so old as to be the mother of our aged teacher could still be alive but such, it seems, was the case. Perched on a wobbly pillion seat on the back of Ruby Brownrigg's bicycle, I was transported the mile or more up to Mrs Fitzsimons' cottage, to be taught my recitation for the Christmas concert. She was blind, but had word perfect a series of suitable poems that we were expected to learn from her to impress our parents with the expressiveness of our elocution.

> *I've got an egg, a nice brown egg,*
> *A nice brown egg for my tea.*
> *I give it a smack, and it goes crack, crack*
> *And sits there and winks at me.*

This was my experience of the oral tradition.

I don't know why I dreaded school. I cannot remember being particularly unhappy there. Unlike in other National Schools of the time, beating was not normal in Ballinatone. I could not match the stories of violent corporal punishment retailed by so many of my generation growing up in Ireland. In fact, I was the only child in Ballinatone ever to be hit, and that was no more than a mild slap from Miss Fitzsimons' chalk-white hand. I was a disruptive pupil, to say the least, with hysterical temper tantrums that no one could do much about. A story was told in aghast memory for years afterwards of how my mother had to sit on me to stop me escaping out the door of the school into which she had just delivered me.

I contrived to stay away as often as I possibly could. I would wake up with the threatening discomfort of the prospect of school somewhere in the pit of my stomach. It became a stomach ache; it really was a stomach ache, I couldn't go to school, I was sick. If my mother was persuaded, I nestled into the bedclothes, cherishing the sense of my sickness. As the noises of the house below, the road outside, told me that 9.00 was past, 9.15, 9.30, and the time arrived when it was not thinkable I could be sent to school, the sickness began to dissipate. The inward chant, 'I cannot go to school today, I cannot go to school today' died out and was replaced by a sense of guilt: I *wasn't* really sick; I was mitching from school. Getting up, dressing, going out to the yard would be the admission that I had been malingering. Yet it was an admission I was forced to make. I couldn't go on pretending to be sick, disguise my desire for a belated breakfast, the run of the house and beyond.

My absences became so frequent at one point as to get reported to the Guards. The state had a responsibility to ensure that all pupils attended school: primary education was compulsory. Came the day when an eight-foot tall Guard arrived at the door, imposing in his dark-blue serge uniform so suggestive of official retribution, and told my mother that he had been instructed to investigate my non-attendance. The number of times had been duly enumerated when I had not been there to indicate my presence by answering 'Anseo' when my name was called out. 'If this continues, Mrs Grene,' said the Guard, 'your son will be suspended altogether.' It was treated as a family joke that the sanction for non-attendance was suspension from school. But to me the appearance of the Guard was a God-like manifestation of my own guilty conscience about staying home.

The days I did go were not bad, really. I walked along the mile and a bit of the Greenan road that led from Clash to Ballinatone. Yes, I *did* walk. Doubt has been cast on this statement by Eleanor, by my children, even on one occasion by my mother herself. But I know that the times I was taken in the car or on the back of Willie Roche's motorbike—a thrilling time that—were exceptional. The norm was the walk out past the line of cottages, taking the right-hand branch of the Y-fork—the other was the Ballyshane Road—up the rise to the twisty up-and-down bends by the leafy Rectory, along the straighter stretch that ended in the hump-backed bridge and the steep hill up to Brownriggs, until the church came in sight and at last the narrow iron gate leading in to the playground. No other road was ever to be so familiar to me, every bend of it, every tree and bush of it: the puzzle of how one side could be the left when you were going to school and the right when you were coming back, the pleasure of summer when the tar oozed up through the gaps in the gravel and you could squish it with your foot or your finger. Later I rode my bike along this route, whizzing down the Rectory hill, forced to get off to push up the hill by Brownriggs. But, no, I wasn't driven to school through my younger years, I walked.

The best part of school was its surroundings. There was a little gravelled playground with a low wall keeping it from the road, where we occasionally did something strange called 'Drill' but mostly played our own games, Tig or Relieve-io. Behind the school was a grassy patch where more energetic games could be played. The churchyard next door was worth exploring, especially in the autumn when the majestic line of Spanish chestnuts yielded edible conkers, glistening red-brown when you cracked their green grenade cases. Across the road was a hazel wood from where you came back trouser pockets distended with nuts in their single, double or treble leaf housings.

I fought anyone or everyone I could. I was the sort of little boy who was all the more belligerent for his littleness. There was a pleasure in lighting into boys several stone heavier, several years older, feeling the intractable mass of their bodies, even if the result was having one's own body pummelled into the playground gravel or the grass behind the school. You were intimate with the ground in any case from trips and falls, legs and knees always showing the abrasions and scars. But the puppy-like tumbling fights didn't prevent me from being more or less mates with my male contemporaries. (There was, of course, no question of association with the girls, the Lord forbid.)

Norman Cassells was nearest to me in age, and the person I most liked to think of as a friend. To me there was nothing unusual about his name. Norman was familiar to me long before I became aware of a well-known category of castles (spelled quite differently) that belonged to the period of the Norman invasions of Britain and Ireland. I was rather hurt on his behalf when, as an adult, someone burst out laughing at the mention of Norman's name. Norman lived up the lane right behind the school and had a brother and sister, grandly grown-up, who had migrated to independent homes far away—places like Kildare and Canada, equally remote from my Clash-limited perspective. Families with connections abroad were not uncommon; there were Brownriggs in Australia. But I never connected my own travel from America to Ireland with the movement of these glamorous, unseen people to equivalently distant destinations. Norman was just my age, though much my superior in the making of plasticene tractors. I envied him his solidity, his farmer parents, his farmhouse so close to the school.

Billy Farrar lived much farther away than I did, miles beyond Clash in the townland of Coolaflake, which to me had some hidden connection with Gold Flake cigarettes. With Billy I often walked home, or we pushed our bikes together in the Clashward direction of the Greenan Road. Billy was older and bigger than I, and his company was desirable as I approached the line of cottages known (though not to its inhabitants) as Hitler's Row. They were council houses built, presumably, at a time when their derisive nickname would have been topical, and whoever lived there—I could have named every one, Kennys, Macs, Kavanaghs—none of them was Protestant.

Were we persecuted as we walked past? Were we jeered at, stoned? Was a rotten egg thrown in my direction? Probably not, though in the more lurid corners of my memory lurk impressions that we were; rational considerations of unlikelihood cannot quite overcome these spectres of recollection. It was the staring, really, or our self-consciousness that turned it into staring. We went to Ballinatone, we were Protestants, we didn't go to Mass on Sunday like everybody else.

And that degree of difference had implicated within it a claim to social superiority. They were the 'Clashers': I, though I lived in Clash, closer to the centre of Clash than anyone, was not a Clasher, and would never be classed as such. And so every school day, I set out not across the bridge to the Clashers' school but the select, genteel distance to Ballinatone, and made my way back with the protective company of Billy Farrar, through the real or imagined hostility of the cottages to the safe haven of our house next to the pub.

Home from school, a shot known in the family as the 'young refugee' photo

CHAPTER FOUR

The men and the village

Driving the donkey to power the turnip pulper

I t was very much a working farm, though we were not dependent on it for our livelihood. My father had kept on his teaching job at the University of Chicago for some part of the year. My mother had lost her university position, but she continued to write at the Clash kitchen table: her book on Heidegger—in 1957 it was the first monograph on the subject in English—articles for journals, reviews for the *TLS* and odd jobs for extra money, a whole volume of African anthropology translated from German, even the occasional recipe for *The Irish Times*. Book royalties were also a significant addition to the family income, especially after the 1959 publication of *The Complete Greek Tragedies*, of which my father was co-editor and translator. But it was no Marie Antoinette-like playing at country pursuits—too muddy, too much manual labour, too intimate a relation to the land for Petit Trianon rusticities.

The yard was always muddy, and the yard lapped right into the kitchen on the men's boots. Three times a day, six days a week, the three workmen made their way into the kitchen for breakfast, dinner (midday) and tea (6 o'clock). Apart from the occasional remark about the work in hand or the weather, they sat and ate in silence. My mother used to be infuriated by the way they waited to be served their food by her instead of helping themselves, as though in token of their male rights, but it was probably just what was considered to be good manners. Neither she nor Mrs Corrigan, who worked for her in the house, ever sat down to meals with the rest of us. The table held six comfortably: with my father at the head, Rufus and myself on either side of him, the cowman and herd Tom Corrigan, a ploughman—a job occupied by a succession of different people over the years—and generally a third, less skilled worker who shovelled and swept at need.

I learned years later that ours was accounted an admirably democratic place of work because we shared the same meals at the same table. There were farmers who kept separate tables for the family and the workers, and these visible markers of hierarchy were much resented. But my parents were always addressed as 'Mr and Mrs Grene', while the men were always called by their first names. Mrs Corrigan, by contrast, was never anything but Mrs Corrigan. I am not sure I even knew her first name until long after I was grown up; she had been ill and she told me how nice it was that she was called Mary by the nurses in the hospital. My parents were thought of as good employers: my father had shocked the small farmer community by paying above the minimum agricultural wage of the time—£3.10 a week sticks in my head as the figure. Still, no one watching those glum, constrained meals in the kitchen would have had any difficulty distinguishing employers from employees.

The Corrigans, it is true, were much more to us than workers. Tom, with his lean dark face (Brueghel-like my parents always said) had been a small farmer in his own right until his farm had been repossessed by the Land Commission when he failed to keep up the

Tom Corrigan with dungfork in pighouse yard

payments. Living in the council cottages was a come-down for the family, as Mrs Corrigan often pointed out. They were not tied close into the familial criss-cross of intermarriage and interrelationship of virtually all the other cottage-dwellers. Tom was a gifted stockman who worked for years after the loss of his farm as a drover for a local cattle-dealer. The long irregular hours of the life—following after cattle and sheep, attending at fairs and marts—suited him better than the more settled routine of tillage. He would turn out to hand-milk our ten or twelve cows morning and evening, six or even seven days a week. He would spend the rest of his time travelling the farm with a little donkey and cart with fencing materials, sticking a bush in one gap and a thorny *sceach* in another. The problem was the other hours, which increased as the years passed, seated in melancholy contemplation of a bottle of stout in Phelan's bar. Tom was not a drunk; his weakness indeed was that it needed a very few drinks to leave him less than fit for work. My father admired him and trusted him, and for the most part Tom repaid that trust with devoted commitment.

Tom was a somewhat remote figure to us as children, thin, silent and unsmiling. Not so the rest of the family: large, garrulous Mrs Corrigan and her three splendid daughters, Daisy, Lil and May, the last two conveniently almost exactly the same age as Rufus and myself. 'Hurray, hurray, hurray—Daisy, Lil and May!' was our rhymed chant when Mrs Corrigan brought them along to work with her. Lil with increasing regularity became her mother's fellow-worker, in due course taking over her household jobs and a great deal more around the farmyard as well. Rufus and she got on very well, though with an edge of uneasiness on Rufus's part that she did not *have* to do the work that was expected of Lil as an extension of her mother's labour—expected of her by her mother, not by us.

May was my first best friend. The sexual apartheid that prohibited male/female companionship at school did not prevail at home. It no doubt helped that May did not go to the same school as I did. The Corrigans' was a mixed marriage; Tom was Protestant and his wife was Catholic. As a by-product of the (from a Protestant point of view) infamous *Ne Temere* decree of the Catholic Church, the children were all brought up in their mother's faith. Some confused notions of her father's religion must have come down to May, for she looked shocked one Sunday when she found me digging industriously in a heap of sand. Did I not know, she asked in tones of horror, that this was work, and for a Protestant like myself to work on a Sunday meant certain hellfire?

Mrs Corrigan, I often thought, taught me more than anyone I ever encountered, with the exception of Tom Cullen and my mad Latin teacher, Mr Pope. I used to spend hours together with her as she cooked and scrubbed and polished. She showed me how to wash a stone floor: first the wet cloth doused in the basin of soapy water, then the cloth well wrung out to dry it off. For mops she had nothing but contempt—hands and knees and plenty of elbow-grease was her prescription. (I cannot have been the only child who thought Elbow-Grease was a patent cleaner like Ajax or Vim.) She taught me to iron shirts: cuffs and collars first, then the sleeves, before spreading out the back and ending up with the tricky strips containing the buttons and the button-holes. Her favourite oaths of emphasis—and there were many of them in her continual stream of talk as she worked just as continually—were 'By the good stick' and 'By the living farmer'. From her I first heard of the little red lane along which food travelled from the mouths of good children. I tried in my turn to make the learning process a two-way one.

When my father fed me occasional words of Greek, I fed them on to Mrs Corrigan. 'βους is Greek for cow' I would tell her. '"Boots" the word for cow—that's a queer class of a language.' She would pretend to mishear so that the game of would-be teacher and dense pupil could be played out for all it was worth.

We were in touch with the village through the Corrigans. My mother was drip-fed village gossip by Mrs Corrigan: the more or less disreputable lives, the illegitimate children, the internecine feuds, who was slipping down the jealously guarded pecking-order and who was getting bumptiously above themselves. The drip-feed could be distracting. For some reason my mother never worked in the sitting-room but always at one end of the kitchen-table, and stories of the Macs and the Hopses (Macdonalds and Hopkinses) must have taken her mind off Heidegger. But she listened all the same. And we, who were always at a sort of remove from the village and the villagers, were vicariously involved.

In it, but not of it. The life of Clash came in to us at second hand through the Corrigans who were part of it. We lived in no big house at a comfortable gentlemanly distance from the farmyard and the smell of the manure heap—the mud did come into the kitchen from the yard. Mrs Corrigan and Lil, who cooked and cleaned in the house with my mother, fed pigs and calves with my mother outside as well. The distinctions and demarcations of a more elaborately stratified world of work and leisure were not for us. Yet all the separations were still there: landowner and workman, Protestant and Catholic, the overeducated and the undereducated.

CHAPTER FIVE

The Farmyard

Shorthorn cows in the farmyard, including White Cow and Dublin Roan

My father's decision to do without tractors wasn't totally quixotic. My parents had owned a tractor in America, though there too they had driven teams of horses. In 1950s' Ireland some, but by no means all, farms had tractors, and workhorses were still much in use. The principle was to resist the inevitability of mechanization and, even more, the dynamic of bigger = better. The machine companies in the RDS Spring Show had an obvious interest in convincing farmers that their latest, largest tractor-driven plough or corndrill was an absolute must for the modern farm. This resulted, according to my father, in small farmers buying machines for which they had no adequate use, having to go in to agricultural contracting to pay off the hire purchase instalments.

It was an argument that would gain credibility again in a later era in relation to developing countries: low-tech, low capitalized reliance on locally available labour and power. But there was always an element of special pleading in these rationales for my father's anti-mechanical crusade. The truth was he loved horses, as he loved all animals, and never cared for any kind of farming in which animals had no part. So tillage, yes, but only tillage with the instrumentality of the horse. If there was no relationship with a living being, then farming became a dead thing. Crops in and for themselves left him cold; vegetables he positively disliked. Beasts were for him the heart of the matter: beasts raised for milk, meat or—still better—trained to human use in work or pleasure.

We had a shifting population of horses, anywhere between four and six. There was always at least a pair of plough horses, even if one of them (a particular favourite called Patsy) was a half-bred mare who served many other purposes as hack and hunter. There was often another carthorse or two, and some riding-horses, cobs, ponies and young horses in the process of being broken. Another of my father's peculiar practices, from the point of view of neighbours, was his willingness to buy and sell from Travellers. Against the general suspicion of their dishonesty, he claimed that they were no more inclined to cheat than anyone else who dealt in horseflesh—a fairly wide latitude I have always felt—and he was never stuck with a horse he bought from a Traveller.

The yard was always alive with animals. Adjoining the house was the stable, with places for five horses: four stalls and a loose-box. The more restive of the carthorses could be heard stomping through the wall of the sitting-room. Beyond them was the long outhouse, the original thatched dwelling-house that antedated the existing two-storey structure. This was where the calves lived through the winter, with successive layers of straw trampled into a deep litter of dung cleaned out in a single Herculean spring evacuation. Early boyfriends of Rufus were recruited for this sort of heavy work—'shovelling shit'

My father harnessing horse to trap

as one put it with an English coarseness that mildly shocked us.

At the top of the yard on the left was the cowhouse, much expanded and improved under my father's management so that eventually it could hold twenty-four cows. Liquid milk, shipped daily for the Dublin market to the splendidly named Tel-el-Kebir Dairies, was the farm's main product. The sights, sounds and smells of the cowhouse remain as the daily bread of memory. Each cow had her own stall, and walked peaceably in when driven from the field, standing in place waiting to be chained up. The Shorthorns that made up the bulk of the herd were sufficiently varied in colour to be easily identified, unlike the interchangeably black and white Friesians that replaced them in my father's later Cavan farm. There was the large White Cow—known by no other name—with her upturned horns, that stood in one corner of the first house: the cowhouse was divided in two. There was the Dublin Roan who stood in another corner. When my father went away to Chicago for the winter, my mother faithfully photographed the cows—rather than us children—and dispatched the snaps to him: whole photo albums feature their pictures, their names and identities mostly now forgotten.

The rattle of the chains as the cows were tied and the clink as their heads went down to eat the rolled grain in their feeding troughs were the background noises that preluded the milking. Then came the initial sharp pinging of the milk streams hitting the bottom of the tin buckets, with the softer sounds as the milk rose up and the successive squirts lathered up into a surface of suds. Such at least was the effect with the experienced milkers—Tom Corrigan, my father, Lil later on. When one was a beginner, the painfully slow drops of milk, tugged from the teats, yielded no more than a flat white plane discoloured with the flecks of dirt dropped from the cow's belly. All the same, there was a triumph when the cow was pronounced done—the teats checked dry by one of those stronger-wristed milkers—and you could make your way to the dairy, the dank and cool little concrete shed just down the yard from the cowhouse, and pour your hard-earned bucketful through the aluminium strainer with its fine mesh filter-paper into the heavy ten-gallon can. With each bucket added you heard the changing sound of the milk splashing down, until the tricky time when the can was almost full and you had to pour it in very gradually, watching out in case it overflowed.

The best time came in winter when the cows were kept in overnight and fed hay after milking. Two doors opened directly from the

Coming from the cowhouse

cowhouse into the adjoining hayshed, and huge forkfuls of hay were dragged through to be shared between the cows, which stood two by two in joint stalls. Contentment and completion were there in the smell of the hay, the chomp of the cows digging into it, and then the long slurp as they sucked up the water from the two-gallon buckets we carried in to them before we had self-service drinking-cups plumbed in. Cows could drink a lot of water, six or even eight gallons, and we exclaimed in amazement as two-gallon bucket after bucket was emptied. And then the special pleasure of the bright electric lights of the cowhouse being switched off, and of stepping out into the darkness, with the light from the kitchen windows nestled down in the lower yard sufficiently near to light us in to tea and warmth.

An animated farmyard it was: across from the calfhouse was the big long horse trough that flanked one side, fed by the overspill pipe from the water-cooled dairy; then there was the boilerhouse with its huge round cauldron where potatoes were boiled for the pigs and the pighouse beside it, with its close-covered ceiling insulated to keep the new-born bonhams warm; houses and pens for other pigs, for ducks and hens, spare horses and ponies. At the bottom of the yard, as important in its way as the cowhouse at the top, was the barn. On the ground floor there were the bags of bought-in feedstuffs, concentrates, linseed and the like, which were used to add protein to the grain. There was the dusty sack-chute down which the rolled barley or oats descended from the hammer-mill in the loft above. The barn was used as a general store in which almost anything could be found, or more often could not be found: buckets and basins, ropes and rodenticides, pieces of old machinery, the accumulated detritus of things that were bound to come in handy some day, though no one knew just for what. On the loft was stored in heaps the loose grain that provided the bulk of the animals' feed through the winter. The loft had to be strengthened with extra beams to support the weight. To keep the grain from spoiling or sprouting, it had to be turned on a regular basis, moved shovelful by shovelful from one part of the wooden-planked floor to another. As often as not, there were the tell-tale black seeds of mouse dung and tiny holes in the wooden skirting-boards that needed to be blocked.

I can remember relatively few of the traumas of a rural childhood, the *Death of a Naturalist* disillusionments of the farmyard. We did kill a pig once, but only once; I have a vague memory of the preparation of boiling water and a vast quantity of intestines later on, but I imagine that I stayed well clear of the blood and the squeals: I was always a squeamish child. The farmyard was for me a place of pleasure that I could call work—helping to feed the calves, collecting eggs warm from the hens' behinds or hunting them in hiding-holes when they laid out, watching the thin stream of cream coming from the separator, the slosh of the butter being made in the wooden churn. At my most energetic I might try to sweep down the yard, propelling the heavy-bristled brush with its accumulating dam of mud towards the side-gutter. It is hard to reconstruct this much lived-in, trodden-on, shat-upon space now when it is all grassed over and I walk up and down with my suburban lawn-mower between outhouses that

contain nothing more animate than firewood, when the loft has been converted into my booklined study, the barn into bedrooms and a whole range of henhouses and pigsties has been replaced with the granny flat. But then the small boy with the irrepressibly sticking-up hair, standing in stripy T-shirt photographed beside the henhouse, is equally hard to discern in the greying sixty-something professor of English who now looks back at me out of the mirror.

CHAPTER SIX

Farming

My father on horse-drawn disc harrow

The house and yard were at the bottom of the hill; on the farm virtually every way was up. The horses strained up the first steep stretch of road out of the top yard gate, their carts piled high with dung, forked from the dungheap opposite the cowhouse. After the sharp left-hand bend on the Whaley Abbey road, the gradient was gentler for a while but after that there was the long slow haul up to the Top Fields, up through successive plots of ground named for long-dead occupants: Kavanagh's Meadows, Hopkins's Field, Carty's Far Field, Judy's Meadows, Thom's Field. Some were less dead than others: one neighbour could remember old Mrs Murphy of Mrs Murphy's Bog and her constant war with Willie Woodbyrne over her thieving goats. He could remember too

Hugh Carty (alias McCarthy) and could explain what was to me the puzzle that Carty's Far Field was nearer to our house than the other top fields beyond it. Carty's farmhouse had stood up above our land—you can still see the ivy-covered ruin in the remains of their yard now surrounded by forestry. When Hugh died in 1933, the nephew who was his heir refused the inheritance because the cost of the ground would not have left it worth his while to farm it. And so the land, which included Thom's, Judy's and what was, for them looking down from higher up the hill, their Far Field, was sold to the State Forestry and came to us as part of a swap effected by our predecessors in exchange for some fields of bog originally mapped on what became our farm. Every named field that the horses trudged up with their cartloads of dung bore the vestiges of lost lives.

There was continuous rotation of crops so that it was only by the quirks of memory that I associate the Top Fields with turnips and mangolds, for instance, the root crops that most needed dung, making necessary that long traipse for the carthorses and their loads. The fat black lumps of dung with the shards of lighter coloured straw thatched through it lay along the valleys of the drills before they were folded back by the drill-plough, moulded into the final straight-formed ridges in which the mangold or turnip seeds were planted. When the little green seedlings were well up, running in continuous thickly planted rivulets along the centre of each drill, there came the thinning. Slow, clay-bound, knee-scraping or back-breaking work it was, depending on whether you knelt or stooped, but sufficiently unskilled that even I could do some of it. Every few inches, one seedling, the strongest and fullest-grown in its clump, was chosen and all the rest mercilessly removed. It always seemed so wasteful to see the multiple corpses of the discarded plants dying out on the side of the drill, the fortunate bedraggled few left to grow and prosper. But before the advent of the precision seeder that could sow one seed at a time, it was the only way to ensure a regular and properly spaced-out crop.

You could tell the mangolds from the turnips by their glossier leaves, though sugar-beet, when we grew it once or twice, had a similar gloss. Within the drills, under the bushing foliage, the roots rounded and fattened, provided they were weeded or 'grubbed' often enough. The grubber was a splendid machine that was driven between the drills, cleaning out the weeds as it went. Handweeding was the unlovely alternative, just as uncomfortable as thinning but much less satisfying because you had less to show for your work as you reached the end of each drill.

In the 1950s there was no mechanical option available to the hand-pulling and snagging of the turnips. Pulling was not that hard; the roots came up out of the ground without much effort. But snagging—trimming the turnip, beet or mangold, chopping off its tops with a sharp, straight blade—was not a job to be given to a child. It could hold dangers enough for adults: on one occasion thick, strong, decent Ned Hops, who was the perpetual butt of his fellows, was so goaded by the man working with him that he snagged his tormentor's hand. It didn't turn out to be more than a flesh wound but it made the point that, even with Ned, you could tease too far.

The other labour-intensive late autumn job was digging the potatoes, associated in my mind with the Three Acres, one field down from Carty's Far Field. (The Three Acres held more than three acres: more like five, the name was down to the 'Irish' acre, larger than its official counterpart, the 'statute' acre.) A machine was used to unearth the spuds, flattening the drills and spraying out a scatter of brown (Golden Wonders), pink (Kerrs) or dark-blue (Aran Banners) across the fresh clay. Then the men, women and boys followed on, picking into wide shallow wickerwork baskets that were emptied in turn into sacks or tipped into a big heap to be 'clamped' for the winter— the clamp being a pyramid of potatoes buried under a thick covering of earth to protect it from rats and frost. But the frost was often already there when we were picking. On a late October afternoon fingers were cold indeed before the fading light forced us to leave the opened potato drills in the Three Acres.

If my memories of root crops, turnips, beet, mangold, potatoes are located in the upper part of the farm, I recall corn, oats, wheat and barley more in the middle ground. Here too there were historically based names—Weekes's Field and the Lime Kiln Field—but others were merely descriptive: the Bank Field, the Holly Bog, the Briary Field. The Bunch of Holes was named for its multiplicity of rabbit burrows that made it nothing but a bunch of holes. Over the years I have seen these names change as names of convenience replaced those traditionally received: the Lime Kiln Field, called for some lime-burning activity of many years before our time, has become the Holly Bog Field by association. The large Bank Field (confusingly) turned into the Lime Field because it was the most convenient place for the large lime lorries to drop their loads. In the turnover of farming activity names come and go within a generation.

My role in the spring sowing season was the humblest and last, that of seed-harrowing. I never learned to plough, where it was essential that you should be able to drive dead straight along the furrow, holding the plough handles steady, with the ropes running through your hands up to the bits on the horses' winkers to drive them on slowly and stop them instantly at the first feel of a rock against the point of the ploughshare. I could only watch with admiration the clean curve of the newly turned sod coming away from the plough, the gleam of the uncovered earth, the shouts of the seagulls as they followed the furrow for worms. When slightly older, I was able to do some of the readying of the ploughed ground with the disc harrow, on which you sat above the sharp circular discs slicing up the ground below, or the spring-tooth harrow behind which you walked, watching the hooped tines drag through the earth. With the sowing itself, I could only assist on the sidelines, helping to empty the sacks of artificial granulated fertilizer into one line of boxes on the seed drill, or again (less frequently) the seed itself into the complementary row of boxes with their separate lids, imagining the fall of the fertilizer and seed together down the long corrugated tubes that led to the metal mouths opening in lines just below the clay. Straight driving, precise control of the lever that shut off the drill at the headland, were essential: otherwise, there were all too visible gaps in the crop or the telltale thicknesses of double seeding. Seed-harrowing, however—the covering over of the seed with a light flat harrow—I could manage, manage even with my own pony harnessed to the harrow. I can still visualize my ten-year-old self in the (to me) vast expanse of the Weekes's Field walking up and down behind the hog-maned Ginger, following the darker earth track of the last line of my harrow.

The most striking change in harvesting since my childhood has been the change from a multiple to a single operation. Now, once the corn is ripe, the combine eats up the field, the grain discharged from the two-ton tank on the machine into waiting tractor trailers in which it is drawn straight into the grain merchant's mill in the local town. A day does it all. Not so fifty years ago. A man with a scythe came first to 'open' the field, cut a single stroke to let in the mechanical reaper-and-binder; the scythed grain from this one stroke was then hand-bound into sheaves. The binder was a separate machine pulled and driven by a tractor, on which sat an ancient man called Dick Ratcliffe whose function in the cutting and binding of the corn I never did understand. The binder threw out the sheaves tied with the bright yellow binder twine that, recycled, was to become the omnipresent multi-use material holding together every part of the farm. Once a few strokes had been completed, teams of helpers could start to 'stook' the sheaves, standing them upright in groups of six, with the heads of the corn a fringe of hair at the top. This was work any of us could do: the sheaves were light enough for the youngest child to drag to the stook. Oats, with their heads showering white with single grains, were pleasant enough to handle. Barley, with its rough beards that cut and clung to you, left bare arms

Standing with Rufus among the stooks

and hands scissored with small cuts, socks a perpetual irritation of itches. (There is a scene in Lawrence's *The Rainbow* where Will and Anna stook sheaves in the moonlight; it is wonderfully evocative on the rhythm of the work but, farm-reared pedant that I was, I used to suck in my breath with disapproval at the idea of stooking sheaves already wet with the dew.)

When the stooks had stood in the field drying for some time, a week or so perhaps, it was time for stacking. Many stooks went to the making of a stack and one of the first harvest jobs I remember doing was to pull in the stooks to the stack-maker. The sheaves were built round upon round into the circular stack until it was tapered off into a top-knot of inverted sheaves, their cut ends bristling above, bound together with a twisted rope of straw. An Indian wigwam was always what they reminded me of, not that I had ever seen an Indian wigwam.

The corn was relatively safe against the weather in its stacked form, so drawing it into the hayshed could wait until there was a space from the pressure of other autumn work. Again each sheaf had to be handled, taken from the stack, loaded on to a low bogie or flat cart, built up in to a balanced load, roped down, and carted in where it was built into a mow at the front of the hayshed—the front of the shed, because the back by that time of year was already full of hay.

Haymaking, the other protracted process of 1950s' farming, happened earlier in the summer. In June the hay would be cut with the horse-mower on which my father sat up, presiding over the fierce blade with triangular knives shuttling on its track through the grass. I would walk along behind looking at the flowering clovers, the thistles and the strong rye-grasses that would fall on the next round, aristocrats to the moving guillotine of the mower. Then there was the stirring of the swath by side-delivery rake or tedder, scattering the green grass, letting in the air and sun, turning the sappy stuff that lay flat and even in the neat rows left by the mower into the messy, crackling cumulus clouds of drying hay. They always get it wrong when they talk about the sweet smell of new-mown hay. It is the smell of two-days' mown hay, hay that has felt the baking of the sun and been scourged by the tedder, that has that sweetest of all scents, making you feel you know what it is to have the appetite of a cow.

The hay too had its long, laborious set of work practices. When it was thought dry enough, and the weather looked set to hold—that was always the gamble—it was gathered into windrows. This was a job I loved. Seated high above the huge round tines of the rake, in the dignity of command over the horse between the shafts, you watched the rake fill up below you with the curving skeins of hay as you drove along the stroke, leaving a clean green path behind you. Then, at a key moment, you stamped on a pedal and the tines sprang up, leaving a beautifully curved roll of hay. The pedal had to be stamped at the same point on each stroke so that each successive roll lay side by side in windrows covering the field.

When the field was all rowed up—no more than a one-boy job— gangs of people appeared to cock the hay. One person, generally my father, raked in to the cock using a sweep, a flat wide-toothed wooden or iron rake that slid along the ground pulled by a horse. The skill was to weave along the windrow, gathering now to one side, now the other side of the rake, until the great mound before you could hold no more. Then you brought it up to where the cock was planned and, with the rope reins driving the horse looped behind your head and shoulders, bent forward and tripped up the rake so that it tumbled over, leaving its yield of hay behind for the cockers.

With a roughly round base established, the cock rose by successive forkfuls of hay dug out of the rake-heaps, bedded and levelled down. A group of two or three people would work at a cock, and if there was more than one batch working, there would be competition to see who could get finished first. The great disillusionment was to come into the field a week or ten days after the cocks had been made. Those magnificently shaped high conical piles of delicately pale green hay had squatted down into little brown hillocks or, even worse shame, if you could identify that they were your cocks, had fallen down altogether. (Christy Mahon in *The Playboy of the Western World* is reproached for building up a cock 'like the stalk of a rush', so narrow it was bound to fall down.)

'Heading' came next: the careful pulling of the butts of the cock, combing it down, and using the loose hay to re-coif its top, after which it had two twines applied to secure it against the wind. Finally the

My father raking in hay to haymakers building cocks

bogies were dispatched to the fields to bring in the cocks. The low platform of the bogie could be tilted at the switch of a lever, so that the end might be backed in under the base of the cock. A suitable small person like myself stood on the back to keep the platform tilted down while my father reversed the horse in against the cock. Long thick ropes were unwound from the front of the bogie, arranged around the back of the cock, and fixed with iron clasps. Then came the exciting part. Working a wooden lever, ratchet by ratchet, the whole cock, some four hundredweight of hay, was dragged up on to the smooth wooden floor of the bogie. At a critical point, when the cock was all but loaded, the bogie floor would tip level all on its own and you heard that tremendously satisfying click that said you were in business. There was roping down, and sometimes if the cocks were small, the tricky business of repeating the operation with a second cock. At last came the glory time of sitting atop the cock, atop the bogie, as it lurched and swayed its way down the road to the little paddock behind the hayshed.

The cunning feature of the hayshed was that it, like the house, was built up against the hill. That meant you could unload the hay from above, pitching the hay down through an opening in the back of the shed rather than having to pitch it up from in front. The bogies were backed into this open mouth of the shed, going very carefully on the slope to stop the whole shooting-match—load, bogie, horse and all—sliding down irretrivably into the pit below. The weathered outer skin of the cock removed, the worry was to see how much damage the rain had done, how far down the telltale signs of heating caused by the damp would go: the stiffened flakes of hay, the discoloured blotching of white and blue and brown, the steam and stench of rot. The good news was a flat yellow-green, perfectly preserved dry hay.

Thrown down into the mow in huge forkfuls, it was dragged to the various parts of the bench that were built up stage by stage. My role here was to stamp down the loose hay, levelling it into place,

With my father and Rufus after a successful loading of cock on bogie

firming it up, always, as the mow rose higher and higher, with the thrill of danger as I tramped along the precipitous edges. Then, with the last cocks coming in, when the hay had reached right up against the corrugated iron roof, and the approaching bogies could be no longer seen, heard only a series of muffled noises, a small body could be used to stuff the final forkfuls up into the remaining space, the heat of the iron overhead, the engulfing hay threatening to close you in. Dusky with dust, sneezing from the hayseed, you crawled down from this last eyrie of the hayshed, convinced that, without your efforts at stuffing and storing the hay up to the roof, the cows would have gone hungry that winter.

When the hayshed was heaped high, the hay behind, the corn in front, in the shortening days of October came the threshing. But threshing has to have a chapter to itself.

CHAPTER SEVEN

Threshing

The threshing machine at work, with horse and cart drawing sacks away to the barn

It was the set-piece occasion of the year, though it might last no more than a day or two. It was the farming event my mother loved most, because she loved the idea of the team, of huge numbers working and eating together. And the numbers were big, maybe as many as twenty-four people engaged in the one enormous multiple operation.

The excitement began with the arrival of the threshing machine, large, high, rectangular, always a delicate off-shade of pink, a wooden structure impressively accoutred with wheels and cogs, a bewilderment of belts. Once it was towed into place alongside the hayshed, the biggest of the belts was attached to a drive wheel on the tractor and the tractor engine started up. With shudders and jolts, crashes and clangs, the vast structure leapt into life. And from that moment, what with the roar of the tractor engine motoring away on the spot, the whir of the belts and the thudding of the treadles ramming the corn down into the mill, nothing under a shout could be heard in the environs of the mill.

Teams of men were assigned to each task. There had to be someone up on the mow throwing down the sheaves. There had to be at least one or two to pitch them up again the four or five feet—it felt twice that to my three-foot high self—to the top of the mill. Up in throne-like splendour, master of the machine, was Liam Clarke, its owner, dark, youthful and curly-haired, cutting the twines on the sheaves, feeding the corn from a table of wood down into the maw of the monster.

How did it know, I used to wonder, how to sort the grain from the straw? I imagined that the seed-bearing heads had to be cut from the stalks, and what mechanical knives could be clever enough to know which end was up. I don't remember how old I was before I realized that all the machine needed to do was to beat the corn strongly enough to shake loose the ripe grain from its husks, what in pre-threshing-machine days was done by the flail. Then riddles took over to do what the winnowers previously did, dividing the corn from the chaff.

The chaff was my earliest responsibility. In the underbelly of the mill was an opening where the chaff came snowing down, a flaky hillock that gradually grew into a mound. My job was to rake back the chaff, to stop it from blocking the chute. Goodness knows if this was a key part of the mill's functioning. Maybe it was just a kindly way to make a small boy part of the work, or prevent him getting himself mangled up in the belts. But I took my job very seriously, raked away with the best of them, and could construct by the end of the day a respectable rick of chaff out of my rakings.

The chaff rick was a mimic Lilliputian version of the straw rick that was being built at the arse end of the mill. Again a whole team was needed, to pitch fork after fork of the bright yellow straw as it came gleaming out from its threshing ordeal up on to the rick, rising on a foundation of brushwood to keep it off the earth of the haggard: one man up at the front of the rick to receive the delivery of straw, one or two to keep building behind. It was harder to build a rick from the loose and light straw out in the open, with the winds of October around you, than to bed down the much denser hay under the canopy of the shed. These were the heroes for me—Chris Reed, Gary Kavanagh—men who did not ordinarily work for us except on this one day in the year.

We needed all the hands we could muster, because there was always the business end of the threshing-machine that had to be manned, the spouts where the corn came out. There were two of these spouts, each with its sack snagged up on hooks ready to catch the flow of the grain. As one sack was filled, and they filled alarmingly quickly, you slammed down a door shutting off that opening, slammed back up its companion, loosing a damburst of grain into the adjoining hessian bag. Quickly the sack was tied—a store of ties cut from the ubiquitous

Building the rick of straw at the threshing

binder-twine had always to be to hand—quickly a fresh sack was hooked up instead, ready to repeat the process minutes later.

Next came the transport of the grain back to the barn. A horse and cart—even a donkey would do—stood ready to shift a load of the filled sacks. It wasn't more than fifty yards, but that fifty yards was more than was comfortable to try to drag a sack full of twelve or fourteen stone of barley or wheat. ('Barrels' remained the unit of measurement: a completely full barrel-sack of oats was fourteen stone, of barley sixteen stone, and of wheat a monstrous, back-breaking twenty stone, but we never filled them that full.) From the rear of the cart a rope on a pulley eased up a sack at a time to the floor of the loft: I can still feel the burn of it on my hands from the time when, in a burst of bravado, I slid down the rope at the end of the day.

For, when at last I was promoted from the lowly part of raker of chaff, this was the eminence I reached, wheeling the sacks unsteadily back from the door of the loft to the heap at the back where they were emptied and piled. The sack-trolley always wobbled and creaked on its little iron wheels, the heave of the sack up to a wheeling position was a heavy pull. But there was no question: this was a real job, an essential job, no mere token chaff-chasing.

It was a sort of popularity contest, the threshing. The custom was that each farmer would donate a man or more to the neighbour who was threshing. But there were farms where men were reluctant to go, farms where the food and the drink were known to be scarce. Once again, my parents' impulse towards the excessive, their dread of the frugal, produced crates of Guinness in numbers to bring in the troops. Even the men from the State Forestry, on their Saturday half-day off, would file in to lend us a hand.

All through the day the kitchen was kept going. Huge pots of potatoes were boiling from as soon as breakfast was over. From midday on, men were summoned in to the kitchen in relays, six or eight at a time, each to receive his plateful of bacon and cabbage and as many spuds as he could eat. Haste there might be—the urgency of the machine to be kept going was on everyone—but sparing and scrimping there could be none. To run short of potatoes would have been the deepest disgrace. Later, tea might be taken out to the men rather than disrupt the rhythm of the work once again. And of course there were bottles of stout, the indispensable lubricant for dry throats and tiring limbs.

By the time it came to the Harvest Thanksgiving service, it was often hard to find a sheaf unthreshed to decorate the church in the traditional way. It was really all over. Hard to connect the anaemic Protestant singing of 'We plough the fields and scatter / The good seed on the land' to anything of that prolonged trajectory from the tillage of March to the grain in the loft in October. Threshing itself—that was the Harvest festival.

CHAPTER EIGHT
Tom Cullen

Tom Cullen in the fireplace of the Clash farmhouse kitchen

Y ou could always tell him by his ears when the Vizards came round.

The Vizards were a Halloween neighbourhood institution in Clash—I never heard tell of them anywhere else in Ireland; they visited on Halloween and on All Hallows night. After supper on each of the two evenings, the kitchen was cleared, the table moved to one corner, chairs pushed back against the wall. Then we waited. At first there were likely to be little crowds of kids from the village; I made one of them myself eventually. A timid knock at the door, a titter or two, and when you opened, they might even be too shy to come in, standing, in sheepish silence, clad in oddments of other people's pyjamas, with monkey masks bought for a few pence in Rathdrum. One of them might eventually be nudged into singing a song, last year's pop song tremulously recycled. A handful of coppers was kept at the ready to send these juveniles on their way, these mere hors d'oeuvres of the real thing to come.

The real Vizards were adults, grown men and women, mostly the players and supporters of the local football clubs. And when they came, they came in style. It was said that one year the competition between the rival 'crowds' of Vizards was such that one lot hired costumes from Burkes, the theatrical agents in Dublin. But even when they came decked out only in stripy pyjamas and wellington-boots, the women and men cross-dressed and masked, with streamers flying and tambourines shaking, they were a terror and a delight. They stomped their way in to the kitchen with cries and halloos, they took the floor for six- or eight-hand reels, the tambourine and the accordion beating out the tunes. The songs might be no more ethnically traditional than those sung by their younger counterparts, but there was something grotesque about the voices distorted by the hole in the mask, venting the strains of the favourite hit of the day, 'Oh to be in Doonaree' or 'How much is that doggie in the window?'

The invasion of the house was all the more striking because of the attendant audience. By custom no one needed an invitation to follow the Vizards. All that unspoken social divide that kept Clashers excluded on the other side of our hall door for 363 days of the year was suddenly removed and the hall, the door of the kitchen, every available space was filled with the people of the cottages.

One of the last appearances of the Vizards in the Clash kitchen

The Ballinacors were the crowd we all waited for; they were the star turn each Halloween Night. Ballinacor was, for reasons unknown, the name that the Clash GAA club had taken to itself, though Ballinacor was two miles up the valley, Kemmis country. Tom Cullen had been for many years the captain of the football team and was the staffman for their crowd of Vizards. The staff that he bore was traditionally tipped with pampas grass and betokened his office as collector and treasurer of the night's offerings. Once the last reel had been danced, the accordionist squeezed out his last tune, the masked staffman went the rounds, beating his staff with tambourine outstretched for cash: nothing less than a note, a pound or more would do as our contribution to the Ballinacors. Even we as children might be given a half-crown, that solidest of all pieces of money, with its embossed horse standing free, to clink into the tambourine. Well-disguised as the Vizards might be, and the Ballinacors prided themselves on their complete anonymity, Tom could always be distinguished by his large red jug-handled ears. It was a reassuring moment. The hint of threat in the masked strangers, the anxiety of seeing the house so transformed, were instantly taken away by the knowledge that one comfortably familiar face was there behind the mask.

In one sense Tom was a pillar of the community: captain of the football team, which had won two county championships, long-serving member of the Wicklow GAA selection board, a well-known figure in the neighbourhood. Yet he was also in some respects peripheral, or at least atypical, set off in his difference as a 'character' both by himself and others. An older brother in a family of (mostly) unmarried men, Tom developed early on into a bachelor uncle figure. He had worked for years as a regular workman on the neighbouring Ellisons' farm, and spoke always with love and devotion of the 'little man', his first employer, Sonny Ellison. But he preferred the freelance life. There had been a long spell when he made a living out of rabbits, ferreting them out of holes, dispatching them with a quick chop of his hand if the ferret had not already killed them, and selling them on to dealers. He instructed me often on how to choose a good ferret: if you put your hand down into the bag, and the ferret drew blood from your finger, that was the one to buy. (I am bound to say, the couple of times I went ferreting with him, it seemed a less than exciting sport, involving a lot of very cold hanging about waiting for non-appearing rabbits to appear, digging down into burrows in search of lost ferrets.) During the war he had picked fraughans (wild blueberries) and sold them for jam: at least he thought it was for jam—he never knew, and never ate the fraughans himself, didn't know what they tasted like. One particularly fine summer he made all of £12, enough to buy himself a cow.

Tom liked to work for others as independent assistant, mentor or guide. His longest-standing, continuing relationship was as part-time gamekeeper to Canon Luce, the Trinity Berkeley scholar. Tom was first taken on by the Canon when he can not have been more than a boy of fifteen, and he beat the countryside with him winter after winter. A postcard would arrive for Tom each week with the regular rendezvous:

'Whaley Abbey Lodge Gate 10.15 Saturday'. They must have made an odd couple, the tall, spare Protestant divine, stern and humourless (or so he appeared to me as a spectral presence at College high table when I was a Trinity student) with the weather-beaten urchin of a boy who knew every turn and boghole of the rough country where they shot. Tom never handled a gun himself, except to shoot pigeons and crows; at a later stage, when he was in charge of rearing pheasant chicks to stock the shoot, he was suspected of shepherding the grown birds back into the farmyard, rather than have them face the guns. But he used to love the times when, through his sense of the lie of the land and the habits of the game, he was able to raise a partridge or a grouse, a pheasant or a hare for the Canon, and there was a respectable bag at the end of the day.

My father always said Tom had a taste for Protestants—the Ellisons were Protestant—he liked being that bit away from his own people and background. Certainly his devotion to the Canon and his son John, who went on with the shoot after his father was too old for the sport, was life-long. And he found an alternative Protestant patron in Alec Foster, even though Alec had nominally 'turned' by the time Tom met him.

Alec was a rugby player who had been capped for Ireland in his day, headmaster of a Belfast school, the school I was to attend myself later on. After his wife's illness and death when he was in his fifties, he married the much younger Catholic nurse who had looked after her, and converted to Catholicism to make the marriage possible. (I always secretly thought of him in relation to 'The Ould Orange Flute', a song he loved to sing—'He married a Papish called Bridget McGinn/Turned Papish himself and forsook the old cause/That gave us our freedom, religion and laws'.) He retired from teaching after a colourful career spiced up by escapades when in the upswing of his chronic manic depression: it was said that down in Dublin on one occasion, he decided in his cups late at night to go call on his daughter Christine (subsequently Mrs Cruise O'Brien) in Trinity Hall, the all-female student hall of residence. Legend had it that the bars on the windows of Trinity Hall were a result of this late-night call. In his retirement Alec Foster moved south and (whether or not influenced by my father, who had tutored Conor Cruise O'Brien when he was preparing for college), bought a small farm just a short distance from ours. He and my father would sit together of an evening and read *The Odyssey*, taking it in turn to read aloud a passage in Greek and then to translate it: I can recall being banished from the room for the grislier bits of the Cyclops episode or the hanging of the maids by the homecoming Odysseus, the makings of nightmares.

Tom Cullen soon moved into the role of man-of-all work with the Fosters. I never knew if he was paid anything: I suspect not much, since Alec had nothing but a smallish pension and a young second family of three children. John, Mary and Brian, all younger than me but John not by much, soon became my favourite companions, and Tom's presence was an added draw to Fosters; he was a sort of Pied Piper calling children to work. He would make us feel, like Tom Sawyer whitewashing the wall, that it was a privilege to dig potatoes or chop up sticks. Constant encouragement, words of praise—a job completed 'couldn't be beat in the world over'—kept us eager and willing. But it was his company as much as his flattery that bound us to him. There was always the flow of talk, the succession of stories which made work with him a constantly renewed pleasure. I would happily head for Fosters and a day of often quite strenuous labour under Tom's aegis, when my grumpy parents could not persuade me to help at home.

Tom was to become my partner and teacher when I started sheep-farming on my own account in 1965. He taught me to shear, to deliver lambs, to pare back the hoof of a sheep with footrot, to spot a ewe with maggots in the warm days of July: if you saw her biting back at herself, you could tell the maggots were in there. He was my close companion as an adult for over twenty years, so it is now hard to reconstruct my memories of him from childhood.

Tom Cullen at work in the Clash farmyard

A walker, a talker, and an independent man of extraordinary character and charm: that is how I recall him always. Tom never learned to drive a car or a tractor: he walked everywhere. For longer distances in his younger days, there was the bicycle. He had one set-piece story of how he rode from Clash to Killarney with a friend to watch a football match, a long weekend's journey there and back. When at home, however, he travelled on foot up and down the hill to Bahana Whaley, his family's small farm just above Whaley Abbey, maybe a mile across the fields from Clash. He had a round of neighbours' houses where he might call in passing of an evening. 'A traveller', he would say knocking the door, coming into the kitchen to take up his place at the corner of the hearth. He would be offered tea or whiskey or a bottle of stout, hospitality amply repaid in talk. His favoured visiting places might change from time to time, for no discernible reason; it was seldom the result of a coolness or falling-out, though Tom could easily take offence if he felt he had been slighted. Somehow his peripatetic route would alter and a neighbour who had seen him every other night for months would hear the knock and the cry of 'A traveller' much less often.

The talk might be local gossip or market news—Tom was never more in his element than at a fair or mart. Equally, when relaxed over a drink, he would launch into his fund of stories. They were never folk-tales; Tom was not a *seanchaí*. They were always stories of his own life or that of the neighbourhood. He loved to tell of how the family of the Cullens were allowed to stay on in Bahana. It was Buck Whaley himself, the legendary rake of the late eighteenth century, who was responsible, according to Tom. The Whaley estate was to be cleared of Catholics, and the Cullens, who had relatives in Tipperary, were preparing to move away. Old Granny Cullen was dairymaid at Whaley Abbey at the time and a favourite with her master. On the day they were due to leave, as Tom told the story, Whaley himself came up to Bahana. He sat himself down on a stone outside the house and summoned the dairymaid out to him. 'You'll not leave, Mrs Cullen', said Whaley, and the Cullens of Bahana are there to this day.

The triumph of a story such as this allowed no room for reflection on the sectarian prejudice, the appalling arbitrariness of the Whaley policy of eviction. Another member of the same family, 'Burn Chapel' Whaley, was alleged to have taken the bell from the old Abbey that gave the house its name and hung it up in the farmyard to summon the men to work. The landlord's politics evoked no word of outrage from Tom. He was on the best of terms with the small farming neighbours, Ellisons, Radfords, Hannons—Protestants all—whose ancestors must have replaced the Catholics dispossessed by Buck Whaley. The emphasis was on the special favour in which Great-granny Cullen was held and the drama of the last-minute reprieve, the consequences for the family remaining in place.

Grudges, resentments, the memories of wrongs could be held tenaciously enough in other circumstances. One long, tangled account of a dispute over a right of way, a gate put up or torn down, that went back some fifty years, was always concluded with the dark reflection: 'And that, Mick, is not something you forget overnight!' (Tom's hold on names was not secure: I was more often Mick than Nick, and on very grand occasions later on I would be introduced as 'Professor Michael Grene'. 'I think his name is Eugene', he would remark casually of some acquaintance, 'but I always call him Jack.')

It was impossible to pin down dates for the stories, at least not the ones before Tom's own lifetime. So I was never sure whether or not it could really have been Buck Whaley who so nearly banished the Cullens from Bahana. Equally indeterminate was the period of the great tinkers' fight in Clash, as Tom related it. At whatever date in the past, a historical 'once upon a time', tinkers took over the village. The men were away working in the mines, so it must have been at one of the times when the copper mines of Avoca were operating; that was a stop-go pattern that went back to the eighteenth century and continued into the years of my childhood when a Canadian company was licensed to mine there, only to pull out again by the 1970s. Anyway, when the men returned, the blacksmith reddened iron bars and with these fearsome weapons the itinerants were driven out of Clash. Once again, Tom would express no partisanship in telling the story, neither for the Travellers nor for the settled community. I never did learn what had precipitated the occupation of the village. It was the extraordinary nature of the event itself, the vivid extremity of the red hot iron in the hands of the returned miners that held the attention.

For Tom the personal was all-important. He and his family were staunchly Fine Gael, equally resolutely anti-Fianna Fáil. Anyone from County Clare was liable to suspicion in Tom's way of thinking by association with Éamon de Valera. But that political bias had its origin in a single incident. The Cullens were under threat of losing their top fields to the Forestry, which would have reduced the farm—only 50 acres at best—to an unworkable size. Workers had already begun to fence in the land. Tom went to the Fianna Fáil TD Paudge Brennan, an old footballing crony. Paudge said there was nothing he could do. Tom then visited Fine Gael Senator Jim McCrea of Carnew, on whom the Cullens had no special claim. 'Tom', said Senator McCrea, 'I know Blowick, the Minister for Lands, personally and I will talk to him for you.' The next day word came down to the men who were sequestering the fields that the fencing was to be stopped. So Fine Gael got itself a life-long supporter.

His relations with the three unmarried brothers with whom he shared the small family farmhouse were somewhat uneasy. He did not get on with his older brother Jim, who was the stay-at-home handyman of the Cullens, doing the plumbing, building and carpentry. They never addressed one another directly, and Tom referred to Jim always as 'the other man'. Conversation with the other two brothers, Hugh the tractor-driver and machine man, and Andy the much ordered about youngest of the family, were gruff at best, limited to irritable queries or commands. Tom's roving ways meant that he was not always reliably there as part of the small farming work machine. He was acknowledged to have bargaining and buying skills and so he was sent as the family representative to sales and marts. But because he didn't drive, someone else had always to go with him. Tom's passion for acquiring odd and (in his brothers' view) quite unnecessary animals was a trial to his siblings. Dogs, ponies, donkeys, peacocks, ferrets and bantam-cocks had a way of appearing unannounced and remaining to be fed and cared for when Tom was otherwise engaged.

A family of foxes was lodged for a matter of weeks down with us because Tom didn't dare bring them home. Normally fond of all wild animals, at lambing-time Tom used to 'blacken up' against foxes, 'like an Orangeman coming up to the Twelfth', as he put it himself. On this occasion, when a number of lambs had gone missing, Tom had traced a vixen to her den, dug her out and killed her, but hadn't the heart to do away with her eight half-grown cubs. So they became temporary tenants at Grenes until they were eventually sold to a man who was restocking Dalkey Hill with foxes.

My favourite story of Tom and the unwelcome animals at Bahana was the tale of the goat. Tom had brought home a nanny-goat and there was all but a mutiny from the brothers. After much venting of anger, it was agreed that the goat could be kept but under no circumstances was she to be allowed to reproduce. Tom formally subscribed to this condition but waited for his chance. Sure enough, there came an afternoon when all the family were out and the goat was 'wanting to go' in the delicate euphemism. Tom brought his nanny across the hill to a farm nearby with a *pucán*, saw the deed done and returned her to her place. Some four months later, the Cullens became the mystified possessors of twin kids. How could it have happened? Tom looked as innocently baffled as the rest and finally offered his explanation for the immaculate conception: 'Maybe it was a deer.'

Tom could neither read nor write, having left school at the age of ten or eleven. We often used to wonder what he might have achieved as a person of his gifts if he had had more education, and he sometimes wondered too. But his talents were human and vested in the voice, so the skills of literacy, the command of print, might not have significantly enhanced his life. He had a self-confidence and personal buoyancy that left him equally at ease with child or adult, people of any class or background, at least when he was on his home territory. He did not try to adapt to what they might expect of him; he simply continued to behave as the person he was sure he was.

I can re-tell some of his stories, though without the grace of his presence as teller. I cannot at all reproduce the quality of his language. The semi-proverbial sayings that larded his talk when written down sound only quaint and folksy. 'A dumb priest never got a parish', he would say when reflecting that you might as well ask for something you wanted even without great hopes of getting it. He would eye some less than perfectly completed piece of work—a crooked fence or a wonkily hung gate—and remark philosophically that 'a galloping horse would never see it'. (The galloping horse was all too often invoked by Tom and myself when we were working together: we were neither of us very neat with tools.) Someone of uncertain temper was 'up and down like a bottle of stout'. I loved his coinages or what I took to be his coinages. A person with social pretensions was 'very highly sprung'. When Ireland eventually went metric, Tom hibernicized the units of weight that then replaced the familiar pounds, stones and hundredweights: the alien-sounding kilos became 'kilogues'. The charm was in the readiness of the phrasing, the combination of inherited saws and aphorisms with the individual relish for words of the natural talker.

Footballing stories, farming stories, anecdotes of animals, memories of dead friends—these were Tom's regular repertoire. Warmed with a drink or two, he would often end with the formula: 'In spite of everything, I got a great kick out of life.' Indeed he did. And he gave to all those whose lives he touched a distinctive zest and colouring, one sort of model of being in the world.

CHAPTER NINE

Friends and relations

Great-aunt May at the barn door in the Clash farmyard with pointer dog

We hadn't many Irish relations and not many friends. By the time we arrived in Ireland in 1952 my father's parents were dead, and so was his much-loved Aunt Jessie, after whom we were mistakenly to name our daughter Jessica: mistakenly because the true name that lurked behind the diminutive with my great-aunt was Jessadora. Of my grandfather's generation the only survivor was my Great-aunt May.

May must have been an impressively independent woman in her time. Unmarried like all her sisters—my grandfather was the only one among his siblings to marry—she set up a successful typing agency in Dublin. She put aside a certain amount of money to help with my father's college education and invested it with her Tipperary cousin Nicholas in bullocks. My father, as it turned out, won scholarships enough to keep himself without the aid of May's livestock fund, but he always remembered her with fondness and gratitude. So, when she was elderly and beginning to suffer from senile dementia in the 1950s, she came to live with us in Clash.

May had always been extremely devout. So, it seems, was my grandmother; at least Rufus remembers being forced down on her knees to say her prayers every day while we stayed in Belmont Avenue, when I was happily too young to be included in the ritual. May, however, made sure of her place in heaven by attending services in all three available Protestant churches, Church of Ireland, Presbyterian and Methodist, a sort of hedging of her bets in the 'pari de Pascal'. By the time she came to live with us, she suffered from deafness in addition to her other disabilities. Her prayerful addresses to the deity were therefore to be heard all round the house, as she spoke to Him at the volume she thought He needed to hear.

A city woman all her life, May drifted astray round the Clash household and farmyard. She tried to create a suburban-style garden, complete with rockery, in a corner of our rough kitchen garden-cum-orchard. She must have fallen foul of my mother at some point because I remember her passing on the warning to me to be very careful of 'Marjorie's plants', my mother's doomed effort to grow sweetcorn in her part of the space where May was building her rockery. One often retold story best catches her bewildered estrangement from the home in which she found herself. Wandering into the kitchen one day shortly before the midday dinner, where Mrs Corrigan and my mother were hard-pressed getting the meal ready, she enquired with her usual single-mindedness 'Where's

Johnnie?' (The generation-slip so common in May's state renamed my father as his own father John.) 'He's over in Phelans', my mother replied somewhat impatiently, as she didn't greatly care for May's fixation on her nephew to the exclusion of all other members of the family. 'Pardon', said May, unable to hear. 'He's in the *pub!*', yelled my mother in exasperation. There was a crestfallen silence from the pious woman reared amid the cautionary tales of temperance preachers. 'He's a good man', she said at last, 'he'll come back'.

I must admit I found my great-aunt a frightening figure. When I was sitting in the sitting-room by the fire, she would come in and, looking agitatedly at me would say, 'Johnnie'—one further slip back of the generations—'you must take me home to Belmont Avenue.' My father had pointed out Belmont Avenue to me on one of our trips to what was for me distant Dublin. I tried to imagine setting out along the 40 miles of road to take my Aunt May back to my grandparents' house. Time and space bent and boggled under my strained efforts to accommodate my reality to the commanding vision of the deaf old woman who had transformed me into my grandfather.

I have no idea how long Aunt May lived with us: maybe only weeks or months, though it feels in memory like a whole phase of my life in Clash. I may already have been at boarding-school when she died and was buried near my grandparents in Enniskerry, the village on the edge of the Powerscourt estate where they attended church each Sunday. The only other close Irish relation surviving then was my Uncle Jack, my father's younger brother. Jack had followed his brilliant brother to Trinity and seems to have been blighted by the comparison. He was homosexual, a drunken would-be writer who hung out with a literary crowd but never got anywhere with his own writing ambitions. He married a fellow student Joan Dobbyn, who knew he was gay and married him in that knowledge, remaining a faithful companion and support to him throughout their lives together. I had no idea what Jack did for a living, largely because my father never willingly spoke of him: they did not get on. My one memory of him, the one time he visited Clash, was seeing him standing by the fireplace with hands extended to warm himself at an unlit fire. Donal Cruise O'Brien, son of Conor, who was staying with us at the time, declaimed with all the priggish indignation of sixteen that Jack had come only to borrow money from my father. I heard no more until, on a visit home from school, I learned that he had died, and it was only much later that I was told that he had killed himself. He became a sore place of silence in the family, the other being my brother Michael who died when I was too young to remember.

Michael was born with a serious mental handicap—I was never clear just what. By the age of one, it was apparent that he could never have anything like a normal development. Some time later he had to be hospitalized and died when he was only three. My mother would often remember the brief time when she had the three of us together—Michael was two years younger than Rufus, two years older than me—and mourned the loss of the larger family she very much wanted. My father never spoke of him; I literally cannot recall him ever mentioning Michael's name. His memory was so marginal in the family that I never talked about him to Eleanor until not long before we were married, when she was extremely taken aback to hear for the first time about his existence.

Neither of my parents had straightforwardly conventional family pieties. My father was obviously fond of his parents—he called them 'my people'—but not at all close to them. The world of books into which university education had moved him was not one they shared, and he had not much time for their devout Protestant faith. He always said that he wished he could have been born a lapsed Catholic. With only the one brother, with whom he was not on terms, and no first cousins, Ireland as far as my father was concerned was family-free, always excepting the distant cousins in Tipperary.

My mother was hardly more connected to her family, whom my father referred to dismissively as 'Marjorie's bourgeois relations'—rich coming from the lower-middle-class Dublin boy he was himself. There was just one older first cousin of my mother's, Edith Neisser, of whom she was fond and with whom she stayed in touch. Edith, who lived near Chicago, was a popular psychologist who published a number of successful books on family dynamics, and won me reflected prestige many years later with my children because she was acknowledged in their cult book *The Princess Bride*. In the lives of Rufus and myself she was an exotic presence, the source (among other things) of welcome 'pink slips', American dollar cheques that arrived punctually for birthdays and Christmas. Her husband was a wealthy businessman, and he and Edith used to stay in expensive hotels in London where we occasionally met them. Tea with Edith and Nookie Neisser at the Connaught, the grandeur of the surroundings, the strangeness of Edith's butterfly-framed glasses with blue cords, the sallowness of Nookie's Jewish face, all spoke to me of a life of bizarre otherness with which I could feel no real cousinly connection.

As a family in Clash in the 1950s we were hardly better supplied with friends than with relations. My parents continued in contact with just a few people from my father's college time. There was the odd meeting with Hubert and Peggy Butler, part of my father's student circle, though in his time in Trinity they had been older, already married and no longer students. The endless source of fascination about the Butlers was the puzzle as to what they lived off; given Hubert's Eastern European interests, a favourite theory was that he was a Soviet spy, though what there might have been to spy on in 1930s' Free State Ireland is hard to imagine. When, a generation later, I married Hubert and Peggy's niece, Eleanor Lenox-Conyngham, the mystery had by no means cleared up: could their Kilkenny country house, Maidenhall, really have been supported by apples sold in the country market and Hubert's occasional articles in *The Irish Times*?

Michael Farrell the novelist and his wife Francie the tweed designer who had her own business, the Crock of Gold, we saw more frequently both in Clash and in their house off Newtownpark Avenue in Dublin. Fierce and forbidding figures they always seemed;

childless themselves, they were 'not good with children', it was always explained to us. During the statutory visit paid annually to Francie's Crock of Gold stand at the RDS Spring Show, I would stand around looking at her dark, heavy, unsmiling face as she exchanged small talk with my parents and wonder how long before we could move on to something more attractive like the free soup stand. With Michael, the continually recurring subject of conversation was his novel, a novel that he had apparently been working on since my father's student days, and which would eventually appear only after his death in the 1960s as *Thy Tears Might Cease*. Michael Farrell supplied me with my first idea of an author: a swarthy face with black moustache, the struggle with some great intangible work, a losing battle with illness.

A central part in our lives in Ireland was occupied by the Mitchells of Merrion Square. Pic Gwynn, as she had been, daughter of the Provost of Trinity and hostess in the Provost's House even as a student, had been among my father's closest college friends. There had never been a love affair between them; Pic was the girlfriend of my father's room-mate, the mathematician Willem van Stockum. The tragic outcome of the romance, as my father told the story, was a Gwynn prohibition on Pic marrying Willem: there was, it appears, madness in the family. Willem subsequently joined the Canadian Air Force and was killed in the Second World War. In his place Pic married Frank Mitchell, my father's exact contemporary at Trinity, who was to become one of Ireland's leading scientists, a geologist who developed the new field of quaternary ecology. None of that registered with us, however; my father had no time for science of any sort and strongly disliked Frank, who always remained for him the thoroughly unsatisfactory replacement for the lost, adored Willem.

The flat at the top of 63 Merrion Square, which the Mitchells rented from the Society of Antiquarians who owned the house, represented the epitome of urban propriety to me. The Mitchells had a nanny who adminstered six o'clock tea to the daughters, Lucy and Rosamund, and then dispatched them promptly off to bed. The nanny, the tea, the genteel orderliness of the flat, all stood as antithesis to the country cousin ways of Clash. If I didn't literally have mud on my boots when I shuffled into the Mitchells' carpeted living-room, I always felt metaphorically as if I did. Things were not helped by the asymmetry of my father's relations with Frank and Pic. Frank had a reputation for being brusque; colleagues in Trinity often debated whether he or the great botanist David Webb could claim the title of being the rudest man in Ireland. He was hardly likely to lay out his best party manners for David Grene. By contrast, my father loved and mythologized Pic so that, by no intention of hers, she became for us the exemplar of everything that was gracious, tasteful and right. The living-room, on the right of the passage as you entered the first floor of their two-storey flat, was Pic's preserve, where she presided with her crinkly-faced smile, her tightly permed short hair, the warmth and firm good sense of her conversation setting the tone. The dining-room on the other side, a solemn mahogany place only rarely entered and never by us children to dine—we ate in the next-door kitchen—was associated with the frighteningly solemn, heavy-jowled face of Frank, whose characteristic style was dryly monosyllabic sarcasm.

Lucy and Ros, almost of an age with Rufus and myself, were the nearest we had to cousins. It was at least some sort of close kinship: we often stayed with them when we were up in Dublin for more than the day. The bedroom/nursery Lucy and Ros shared was a familiar space to me. And yet everything also was alien—the smells, the sounds, the bathroom with its explosive geyser to heat the water, the little lavatory in its own room at the end of the passage with the high chain to pull. It was all governed by a set of rules and constrictions that cowed and hedged me in, convicting me of my loutish uncouthness. The Mitchells were the measure of how far I fell short of the right way to do things.

My parents developed remarkably little in the way of a social base in County Wicklow. There were the Fosters, the companionship afforded to my father by Alec, John, Mary and Brian as my daily playfellows. Other anomalous presences in the neighbourhood sometimes yielded more or less temporary relationships: Jim Gilbert, a journalist who wrote on farming matters and ran a somewhat experimental and dubiously successful farm nearby at Ballycreen; hunting acquaintances such as John Fletcher, an Englishman, who briefly kept the hounds across the valley from us in Ballyknockan. We were thrown together by our common status as blow-ins. However familiar we were with the small farmers around us, they didn't become 'after-dark' friends: we worked together, we didn't socialize. And, whether by choice or accident, my parents never got to know any of Wicklow's 'county' families, apart from casual contacts through horses.

Of course, my father was away for much of the winter, my mother preoccupied with her own work, as well as with the labour of running a farm and five-month-a-year single parenthood. But friendship for them was a matter of chosen individual relationships, based as often as not on shared intellectual concerns; it was not embedded in the contiguities of a neighbourhood or community. So, even after the move to Clash, the visitors from America were more important to their landscape of people than those among whom they lived. Each summer some of the names that animated my parents' talk when my father returned from Chicago were incarnated as American birds of paradise in our home.

Some were long-term friends, like Bill and Shirley Letwin, among my father's earliest students, who settled in London to become the parents of Oliver Letwin, who went on to front bench positions in the British Conservative Party. A black and white snap of them in Clash, looking unbelievably young, is a prompt for the older, marvellously generous and hospitable couple who were so kind to Eleanor and myself when we wound up as lost and bedraggled graduate students on their Regent's Park doorstep many years later.

Another set of visitors to Wicklow I remember only for the scarlet-making shame they involuntarily caused me. A newly married couple, the unfortunates came to Ireland on their honeymoon. Forgetting entirely that Rufus's bedroom had been reallocated to them, I burst into the room to face Mrs Newlymarried without a stitch on her, the first adult naked woman I had ever seen. I still cringe at the memory of my completely speechless exit. The whole sense of discomfort was compounded by the fact that they broke the—no doubt old and rickety—bed, producing an endless succession of ribald comments from Jim Cullen, who was called in to mend it. I felt culpably implicated in the whole unimaginable scene of sex.

My father was an evangelical apostle for the special value and amenities of living in Ireland. He lured his friends not only to visit us in Clash, but in the case of the von Simsons, to buy a holiday cottage not far from us in Tinahely. Otto von Simson, a colleague of my father's from the Committee on Social Thought, was an eminent art historian, author of a standard work on the Gothic cathedral, with long elegant fingers and a delicate German accent. His wife Lulix was an aristocrat of the Austrian Empire and it was said that when they first moved to America, her only culinary skill was the cooking of rich chocolate torte; there had always been servants to prepare the more everyday forms of food. (For some reason this anecdote always merges in my head with that of another Viennese friend of my father's whose cook turned out to be an arsenic poisoner from a village where the tradition was arsenic poisoning.) Lulix was one of a number of women sufficiently devoted to my father to be described (by my mother) as being in love with him. I certainly fell in for redirected love (if that is what it was) and was petted as 'das liebe, kleine Nicky-lein'. Who could resist that from a Bohemian princess with fine silken white hair about her face? Anyway, for whatever reason, the purchase of the cottage in Tinahely was primarily her doing and she continued to visit there faithfully each summer long after my father had moved elsewhere in Ireland, although she had been outraged by the assertion of the local parish priest that Hitler's misdoings had been much exaggerated: it was no more than 50,000 Jews he had killed. Evidently, the priest felt that this was an allowable number.

The most surprising part of my father's hibernophilia was his belief in the benefits of an Irish education. American friends, harassed by the antics of crazy mixed-up adolescent children, were urged to send them to Protestant Irish boarding-schools. John von Simson, then known by his pet name of Dody, was dispatched to St Andrews, my father's own former school. The son of another friend, Mike Donoghue, found himself in Bandon Grammar School. The crumby, crumbling establishments always just a few pupils away from closure must have been as startled by a John or Mike, as John and Mike must have been disoriented at finding themselves so far from their academic brat peers in Chicago's Hyde Park. Still they survived and prospered, so maybe my father's eccentric educational policy was not so misguided after all.

Maurice Donoghue, Mike's much remarried father, came to stay with us bringing a glossy photo of his latest glossy wife, Virginia, who smiled down dazzlingly from a prominent place on the dresser, her glamorous American stylishness an amazement among the Willow Pattern plates from Arklow. The other memorable feature of Maurice's visit was his gambling. He had apparently never been racing before but, finding himself short of spending money, he set about making what he needed on the track. Each day he would disappear off to one meeting or another, get up the form, seek out the most knowledgeable of the bar-room bystanders, and make his bets. What is more, astonishingly, he won. At least he claimed by the end of the week he was substantially ahead of the game. He set for me a mark of the American, the willingness to do the outré, the improbable, the impossible, and somehow make it work by sheer lack of fear of its foolishness.

Growing up in Clash, I had no fixed sense of what it was to be ordinary. Only of one thing I was sure: we were not it. Ordinary families lived where they lived because their parents and grandparents had lived there before them. They were what they were by virtue of the people to whom they were related, the church to which they belonged, the fastening conditions of set social roles and places. But my parents were, extraordinarily, the people they chose to be, and as a family we lived by those choices, not in a given webbing of friends and relations.

CHAPTER TEN

Ponies

My first pony Sally, and Rufus on Patsy

The Fosters were not a riding family but they had a pony before I acquired one. It was an ancient, shaggy, black pony and for months he did nothing but stand around in a field near their house. They had a winkers for him—the carthorse equivalent of a bridle with blinkers to keep the horse's eyes focussed forward—but no saddle.

There didn't seem to be any point in having a pony if you couldn't ride him, and I felt it was up to me to take the initiative on this one, because mine was a riding family. My father had not had much opportunity to ride as a boy, but made up for it as an adult. With all the zeal of the late convert, he was passionate about horses: riding them, hunting them, working them, driving them, anything but racing them. (Though his admired Grene Park cousin Nicholas, my namesake, had kept racehorses, this was the one form of equine sport for which my father had no time.) There was always at least one riding horse in Clash, and already at the age of five or six I had been put in the saddle.

Very far above the ground it felt up on the mare Patsy's back. Solemn and insecure, I was walked round and round in a circle, trying to remember how I had been taught to hold the reins, with my feet stuck in the stirrup leathers, my legs too short to reach the metal stirrups that dangled and clanked below. Those occasional turns round the exercise field with my father at Patsy's head hardly made me a seasoned rider. Still in the company of the Foster children, who were younger than me and had never so much as sat astride, I was the horsey one and had to live up to my reputation.

So I somehow or other managed to encase the Foster pony's head in the heavy winkers with the straight bit and the rope reins. He stood stock still, lost in the lethargy of old age and inaction. Somehow or other, I clambered up on his long-haired, mud-encrusted, dusty back. Taking up the slack of the reins, clicking my tongue in what I hoped was an imitation of my father's approved manner, I dug my heels in the pony's sides and succeeded in stimulating him into action. Incredulous that such a thing was happening to him at his time of life, the pony moved forward in the slowest of slow walks.

That was the beginning of what must have been a bad time for the old pony, stirred out of superannuated slumber. Every day I arrived at the Fosters, eager for a new stage in my riding career. The walk was pushed up into an ambling jog, an extremely uncomfortable gait for the bareback rider joggled up and down without the aid of the stirrups that allowed a rider in the saddle to 'post' to the trot. The very discomfort of such bareback trotting made me urge the pony on to a canter, which, with its rocking-horse motion, was much easier to manage without a saddle. If you gripped tight with your knees and went with the movement of the pony below you, there was none of the painful potato-sack feeling that went with the trot. And there was the sensation of speed. You could call a canter a gallop, you could imagine yourself moving at headlong, breakneck pace, whatever the actual activity of the galumphing creature you were riding.

Eventually, emboldened by my example, John Foster himself took to riding, and then even Mary and Brian. But my period as lone rider, the daredevil who had leaped lightly on the bare back of the pony, who had shown the others how to do it, confirmed my self-image as horseman extraordinary. I was more than ready for my own first pony when she came along.

She was white and she was beautiful. Of course, I was taught to call her a grey, the standard convention by which those horses that start off as black foals, turn iron grey as yearlings and are completely white by the age of ten, remain greys throughout. For me, though, Sally was white, her whiteness a part of her glamour. My father had bought her from the Travellers in a poor enough condition, wretched with saddlesores that I lovingly anointed with green salve. Clash levels of feeding, however, soon set her to rights. Somewhere or other, a pony bridle and saddle had been acquired, and my bareback apprenticeship was over.

Sally was wonderful to ride, docile, well-mannered, doing just what she was asked. And after the antique Fosters' pony, she seemed immensely young and energetic, ready to canter at will. Now I could learn to trot properly, rising and falling in the stirrups to the rhythm of the gait—smart, alert, dexterously in command. While I was up in the saddle there were no problems whatsoever. But on the ground, it was soon discovered that Sally had one little foible: she kicked.

When she was first bought, she was so malnourished she probably couldn't have managed a kick. But as the oats restored her condition, it restored also her latent evil habits. She never succeeded in kicking me and once I realized that I had to avoid the swing of the iron-clad back hoof, I took to mounting from in front, against the approved fashion. The crunch—or what was nearly the crunch— came when she was being mucked out in a loose-box by Chris Reed. Chris worked on the Forestry but used to do relief milking for us on a Sunday evening, as well as other odd jobs from time to time. He lived in a tiny cottage, possibly once a lodge, at the edge of the Whaley Abbey farm: it now is a ruin covered over with bushes. I can remember vividly his dark, smiling, somewhat monkey-like face—though it wasn't smiling as he told my father what had happened in Sally's loose-box. He had just bent down to pick up a fork, having cleaned her out and bedded her down with fresh straw, when without warning the apparently peaceable Sally hit out. 'She missed my head by that much', Chris illustrated dramatically with his fingers. No question: Sally had to go. And she went—back to the Travellers who had sold her to my father and who of course exclaimed with surprise that they had no knowledge of her hidden bad habits.

Next was Billy, an elderly brown pony, less sprightly, less smart than Sally, but still a cut above the Fosters' old-age pensioner. Billy's specialty was bucking, and a tendency to lie down and roll in ploughed ground. Luckily for me he didn't buck when on the road; but take him into a field and move him past a trot, ask him to do what he didn't feel like doing, and the sharp zig-zag up-and-down motion of the buck started up. Sometimes I succeeded in sitting it out; once at least that I can remember, I was dislodged and came banging down on a specially memorable stone in the Daisy Bank, memorable because it had been bored for dynamite blasting but had never been blasted. Its surgical scar of drill-holes made it a landmark in the field, and I associated it ever after with a fall off Billy and dark talk about concussion for several days after.

Billy might or might not get you off bucking in a meadow or pasture; but when he took the notion in a ploughed field, all you could do is jump off before he rolled on you. To be fair to Billy, quite a lot of horses do this: the clay seems to act as an irrestistible lure. Billy was just my first experience of feeling the legs go under me, the sinking, trembling sensation of the horse going down, the strange sudden proximity of the earth, the helplessness as you watched your nicely polished saddle battered around in the furrows under the animal. It was a reminder that really you had *no* control over the horse that normally seemed to be responsive to your command. The whole riding business depended on the assent of your mount, which he could withdraw at will. If Billy wanted a roll in the clay, that was that.

Billy's little foibles were regarded as tolerable and I cannot recall why, in the end, he was replaced by Ginger. My first sight of Ginger was a real disappointment. She was very small, only just over twelve hands high, she was hairy, she was a chestnut with a hogged mane. My father had bought her when I was already at boarding-school, and I had to repress my sense of letdown when he took me out to the shed and showed her to me. If Billy was to be replaced, I wanted something larger, grander, more befitting my grown-up, ten-year-old self. Ginger was younger than Billy, but in no other respect did she seem an improvement. My father no doubt could sense my lack of enthusiasm but trusted that I would learn to like her.

And sure enough I did. Ginger was with me for the rest of my time as a rider, probably some four years. Spring made her less shaggy; the curry-comb and the body-brush disposed of the mud and surplus hair. The hogged mane was still there but seemed to suit her spiky, obstinate personality. She was self-willed and determined, living up to the general principle that the smaller the animal, the greater the need to assert themselves. When asked to do something she disliked, she would lay her little ears back against her flat-cropped mane and register her reluctance unmistakably. She could be persuaded, though, and we made a good partnership. I too had, if not a hogged mane, an urchin-style crew-cut with sticking-up hair accentuating my widow's peak, and the spectacle of me mounted on Ginger must have been one young tyke on another.

One of the most withering of La Rochefoucauld's cynical maxims is the proposition that you are never as happy or unhappy as you think. Whatever its validity about present feeling, it is no doubt true—if always unverifiable—in relation to the past. How happy was I riding Ginger, hunting Ginger, driving Ginger in the trap or behind the seed-harrow? Pleasure in the ordinary and the everyday can be recollected only by holding in memory some individual instance that stands in generically for its multiple repeated counterparts. Day-by-day happiness drains away into the sands of the passing time. And in the case of riding and horses, positive memories tend to be overridden by later denials connected with adolescent rebellion against my father, in which riding was the issue of revolt.

Still, some sensations continue to ring true as pleasure some fifty years later. There were the smells, the straw, the horse-dung, the leather; there was the briskness of grooming and tacking up the pony: her ears-back grimaces and uneasy shifts of the body if you brushed her too vigorously, the bit negotiated into the mouth, the bridle over the head, the saddle girth tightened and retightened. I have always loved routines, and the routine of getting ready to ride, bringing the pony back into the stable when you were done, were key parts of the experience.

Self-image and fantasy were components also. To ride was to walk tall, even if you were a small boy (notably small for your age) on a twelve hands pony. Riding was as grown-up as you could get at ten. You were after all in control, or at least negotiating control with the animal under you. I longed for hunting-boots with leather running right up the leg to below the knee; I had to make do with low-ankled jodhpur-boots, a very inferior substitute, scarcely distinguishable from shoes. The riding-hat added real glamour, however, its hard surface covered with black velvet, with tiny black ribbons tailing behind, the unexpected opulence of its red-satin lining. The creak of the leather as you moved around in the saddle was the sound of the cowboy on the range, riding out after cattle. I have a shoulder-bag to this day that gives the same creak; as I board my commuter train at Rathdrum, all the reveries of riding return in my head.

I was perhaps happiest just riding out round the forestry tracks on my own. 'Schooling the pony'—that was exercising her under my father's eye in the fields, trotting in figures of eight, left- or right-hand leads at a canter—hunting, show-jumping were all more exciting but complicated by the other emotions involved. In all these, the need to please my father was paramount; you craved his praise, you dreaded his reproof. He yelled a lot—'Heels down, toes up, knees in', 'Left lead, I said *left*!'—he pushed you to do what scared you. But that made the balm of congratulations all the balmier. And he rarely withheld the warm reward of approval.

I only ever hunted twice, neither of them pleasurable occasions in the memory. Most of the time was spent hanging around getting cold while obscure things were being done with the hounds which you couldn't actually see. The grown-ups on their high hunters engaged in desultory conversation that was in every sense of the word above your head. There would come a sudden quickening of pace when the hounds went away, or were thought to have gone away. And that would be quite scary as a whole crowd of horsemen jostled one another at a trot down a lane or through a wood, all seized with the sense of not wanting to be left behind if something was actually happening. But, of course, most of the time, nothing did happen. There would be a check, which meant more hanging around until your fingers felt so numb you could hardly hold the reins.

It wasn't great even when the hunt did get moving in earnest. Ginger got very excited and determined to be up with the best of them, and she had an iron mouth when she took it into her head to go. I have horrific memories of our committing that blackest of black sins on the hunting-field, getting ahead of the huntsman. I seem to recall, worse still, that Ginger once kicked a hound. Even if none of this happened—and years of reading about Trollope's hunting cads may have coloured my memory—hunting lives in my mind as a mixture of boredom, discomfort and shame, for which the tiny bursts of excitement were no adequate compensation.

Better than either of the hunts I actually rode was one that never happened. It was supposed to be a special treat on a half-term I had home from school. There was a meet at The Beehive, the pub near

Brittas Bay, some twelve miles from Clash. My father and I rode over on the Saturday morning in good time for the midday meet, only to discover we had got the wrong day. It was the previous Saturday, or the next. My father was mortified. As we rode back, it was my cue to reassure him that I wasn't too disappointed. And I spoke no more than the truth. I had been let off the dubious delight of hunting, and I had the unalloyed pleasure of my father's company and conversation in the hours spent hacking to and from our non-existent hunt.

The strain was always in the expectations, the build-up, the anxiety of doing well or doing badly. In this, horse shows were the worst of all. All summer long there would be a succession of shows and gymkhanas: in Bray, in Ashford at the Bel-Air Hotel, in Carnew or Tullow, or, biggest event of all, the county show in Tinahely. My mother claimed to have driven back and forth to Tinahely fourteen times one August Bank Holiday Monday. Our full panoply of horses was entered at Tinahely: horses taken from the cart in the carthorse class, ponies and hunters in the riding classes and then in the afternoon the show-jumping. The most humiliating day of my entire life was one Tinahely show when not only Ginger, but also Rufus's pony Buzz, refused three times at the first fence—both of them ridden by me. For some reason my father had decided that Buzz had a better chance with me aboard than with Rufus. It was all one.

We never should have been there. We rode horses bought from the Travellers, ponies with docked manes. They were never groomed right, tacked right. Because Tinahely was the day before the RDS Horse Show, a selection of the professionals were there—famously one year the then famous Tommy Wade with his wonder horse, Dundrum. And lined up outside the ropes of the improvised showjumping ring were the cars of the county, with their hampers and their shooting-sticks, those people whose horses had prettily plaited manes and gleaming saddlery, whose daughters wore their hair in hairnets under their hunting-caps. It shouldn't have mattered, of course, if we had been having fun, but it was all scrambling, pointless rushing about, misery and boredom—boredom above all.

Because when you weren't desperately trying to get your pony to jump or riding round the ring under the derisive eye of the judges, you were always holding some damn horse's head while adults disappeared into the refreshment tent, or walking a horse up and down to cool it off after the exertions of the jumping. Once—my moment of glory—Ginger and I got a third prize in the under 12.2 pony jumping in Bray. Were there more than three ponies entered? I cannot remember. But we did get round the course. Once—my father used to tell it as a story infinitely redounding to my credit—I rode round the jumps in Tullow in spite of having vomited out of nerves a few minutes before. Most of the time nothing so dramatic happened—nothing at all happened.

It wasn't until years later as a sullen teenager that I gave tongue about the awfulness of it all. We were in Cavan, coming back from a horse show with my father and stepmother, Ethel, in the front of the

On Ginger with our third prize rosette

car. By then, I played a wholly peripheral role, back-up groom and stable-boy, as I told myself mutinously. I addressed all my remarks to Ethel in a cowardly sideways attack on my silent father at the steering-wheel. 'Really', she exclaimed in her bright interested manner, 'you've always hated horses. Really—how extraordinary!' I waxed eloquent on the dreadful circumstances that surrounded horse-riding, hunting, show-jumping, the terrible effect that having anything to do with horses had on the character. And at that moment of teenage rebellion, I believed it all and continued to believe it for many years as an article of faith. I felt obliged to get growly at the very mention of horses. Even up to a few years before my father's death, I could get into a fury when required to help tackling his horse and buggy, as he fretted over the way I should be doing what I was doing all wrong.

Did I cut off my nose to spite my father? Could I have been enjoying riding for years if equiphobia hadn't become a point of principle? I suppose any son has to get angry with his father over something, and it may have been better to localize the anger over horses than diffuse it over the whole relationship. But it was an acute version of the central difficulty of being my father's child. He passionately wanted you to love the things he passionately loved: farming, literature, riding. And you loved him enough to want what he wanted. You felt the need to come up to his standards of excitement—half-heartedness, lukewarm participation were detestable compromises. I could have been an easy rider. That wasn't an option; riding could not be allowed to be easy. So I ended up not riding at all.

CHAPTER ELEVEN

Going Away to School

At the crossroads in Clash, kitted out in our Drogheda Grammar School blazers

At nine there was nothing I wanted more in the world than to be allowed to go away to Drogheda Grammar School. Rufus had been sent there—on a recommendation from Pic Mitchell as I remember—after her year's unhappy experience of a convent school in Rathdrum. It was a very small Protestant boarding-school of no more than sixty pupils, small, friendly and informal: that was the story. And Rufus loved it. She came home with stories of the teachers and the children which had me wild with anticipation of the time I could join her there. My sister, with all the dignity of four years' seniority, I idolized. It didn't stop me quarrelling with her constantly, resenting her bullying, crying to my parents when she hit me. But in my heart of hearts she was the very paragon of maturity to which I aspired. So I too longed to be at DGS, to wear its school uniform, to be one of the initiates who played hockey and lived in a swirl of boarding-school intrigue. (Enid Blyton must have helped: I had faithfully read my way through all Rufus's copies of *Claudine at St Clare's*, *Fifth Form at St Clare's* and the rest.)

It wasn't intended that I should go to Drogheda until the autumn of 1957, just before my tenth birthday, but I so pleaded with my parents that they allowed me to enrol for the summer term instead. So there I was at last, aged nine and a half, in the glory of my school blazer with the crest, which I somehow imagined incorporated crossed hockey sticks, proudly proclaiming the date of the school's foundation, 1669. It apparently belonged to the generation of schools established in the seventeenth century by one Erasmus Smith, a London alderman who had acquired large Irish estates as an 'adventurer', and who set

In the grounds of Drogheda Grammar School with our mother

the schools up for the nurturing of wholesome Protestant doctrine. One of the Drogheda Grammar School 'houses', the very superior one to which Rufus belonged, was Erasmus Smith; I was mortified to find myself assigned to the despised Grattan House, presumably named after the patriot, though I know of no connection between him and the school. The third house was Singleton, called after the Drogheda citizen whose extremely handsome eighteenth-century town residence made up a large part of the school.

Of course our 'houses' were not separate living quarters, like those in the British public schools. The school was much too small for anything of that sort: there was only a boys' side and a girls' side, some four or five dormitories in each. The main entrance hall to the school, what must have been the original entrance of Mr Singleton's home, had a beautifully tiled floor in black and white chequerboard marble. At least in retrospect, I realize it must have been beautiful, though at the time I remember it only as a very chilly place where you waited outside the headmaster's study generally in anticipation of some severe reprimand. A fine staircase led up out of the hall to the headmaster's flat on the first floor—a reserved territory visited only on special occasions to watch something suitably edifying, like a production of *She Stoops to Conquer*, on the TV. Once you moved out of this state area—to the right towards the dining-hall and girls' dormitories, to the left through a library down a dim corridor to the next-door house on St Laurence Street, which held the boys' dormitories—you were quickly beyond marble-tiled floors and stair carpets. Bare wooden passages were what you clattered along on your way to your dorm, or trooped down in order three times a day to meals in the dining-hall.

Allegedly the first place of education of Arthur Wellesley, later Duke of Wellington (though no one ever found hard evidence that he had been there), the school had dwindled by the 1950s to the very verge of closure. Then the gifted headmaster, Arnold Marsh, persuaded the Society of Friends to take it over and saved the school from extinction. It did not officially become a Quaker school, like the Friends' School, Lisburn, or Newtown School, Waterford, but many prominent Quakers—Basil Jacob of Jacob's Biscuits, Bevan Lamb of Lamb's Jams—sat on its management committee. And corporal punishment was banned at a time when it remained one of the standard methods of instruction in most Irish schools.

For those who taught there, it must have paid miserably. It was alleged that the English headmaster Eric Brockhouse, who succeeded Arnold Marsh shortly after I arrived in Drogheda, was paid £800 a year over and above his rent-free flat. This was thought to be a princely salary and may well have been inflated by envious begrudgers who did not care for Mr Brockhouse. The ordinary teachers can have been paid only a fraction of that. And of course, as a result, Drogheda got the teachers it paid for. There were 21-year-olds fresh out of college, like Clodagh Grubb, who taught me art and whom I was to meet years later as the wife of a Trinity colleague; there were even those who had never been to college, like Joseph Hone the writer, who served his time there on no qualifications whatsover. There were Evelyn Waugh-style lunatics and eccentrics. One Latin teacher in Rufus's time, Mr Commons, had a violent dislike of girls and hit Rufus over the head with a Latin dictionary. That put an end to Latin for Rufus. In 1956 there were stray Hungarian refugees recruited to teach French, on the grounds no doubt that they were after all Europeans. There were misfits and mavericks of every sort and condition.

My own favourite, the man who taught me more than anyone except Tom Cullen and Mrs Corrigan, was the mad Mr Pope, who replaced Mr Commons as Latin teacher. Mr Pope, who signed all his corrections JRP, though what the JR stood for remained in obscurity, was a one-armed Englishman who had taught, he told me once, in thirteen different schools. That in itself was suggestive, even if I could never make out suggestive of what. He had been a headmaster at one point and from time to time would voice discreet dissent from the way DGS was run. He had taught in boys only schools before and did not approve of co-education: it made the boys sissies and the girls brazen, he told me. He was very religious and had bizarre political views, believing that there was a conspiracy between the Catholics and the Communists to squeeze out the small Protestant nations of the world.

Mr Pope was widely regarded in the school as an exotic if not a grotesque. He had lost an arm in an accident; he explained it all in circumstantial detail, how he had his arm out of the driver's window when it was hit by the inswinging trailer of an overtaking vehicle. The school gossips inevitably said he had drink taken at the time. It was fascinating to watch the strength and skill with which he cut up his food with the knife in his left hand, and then proceeded to eat it with the fork, to follow the empty shirt-sleeve swinging as he played a vigorous game of table-tennis, to see the neatness of the italic hand he had taught himself to write after the accident.

I was, I have to confess, something of a pet of Mr Pope, relatively advanced in Latin (his principal subject), the only pupil to enter the literary quizzes he would set from time to time and pin up on the noticeboard for all-comers. 'Ruin seize thee, ruthless king! / Confusion on thy banners wait' is still all I know of Gray's 'The Bard', but I did track down the lines after hours of hunting through poetry anthologies. (He must have had a taste for this sort of dramatic rhetoric. Dryden was another quiz author: 'Fallen, fallen, fallen, fallen, / Fallen from his high estate / And weltering in his blood'). He encouraged me to read anything and everything; quality didn't matter initially as long as we got into the habit of reading.

Mr Pope taught the sort of range of subjects that any DGS teacher had to—not just Latin, but English and even Maths. And everything he did, he did according to his own individual principles. English class, particularly near the end of term, was turned over to his reading aloud of John Buchan; I can remember nothing now of *Huntingtower* or *The Three Hostages* but the hypnotic pleasure of hearing him read.

All through one winter session, he taught his English and his Maths classes based on an imaginary factory that made a toothpaste called Splosh. In English, we were required to write advertisments for Splosh and how it gleamed whiter than white owing to its special whitening ingredient Gleamo. For the final maths exam, we were set a series of problems. 'If the Splosh night watchman walks at the rate of 50 yards a minute and it takes him 36 minutes to complete his rounds, what is the area of the Splosh factory grounds?' The final sum was to calculate the proportion of Gleamo in a 20oz tube of Splosh, having added up all the other ingredients to the fourth decimal point. The answer: 0.0001%. Mr Pope was my kind of teacher.

I saw him only once after I left school and somehow the special sense of mad magic seemed to have left him. I heard many years later that he had been fired from Drogheda for an attempted assault on the young Matron; maybe this was the explanation for the thirteen schools. I never knew if he got to teach in a fourteenth. He is now long dead: JRP, RIP.

Drogheda Grammar School must have been a pretty poor school, looked at in retrospect. Some pupils evidently got themselves a decent education there and went on to university, but you improved your chances if you transferred to some other school first, as Rufus was to do to Alexandra College in Dublin, and I was to do to Belfast Royal Academy. We weren't notably mistreated, weren't beaten, weren't bullied more than in any boarding-school, but our teaching left a lot to be desired. Small, friendly and informal could have been translated into small, amateurish and unprofessional.

At nine and a half, however, you knew nothing of that. The sixty pupils seemed a horde, an army, to someone coming from Ballinatone with its total attendance of thirteen. The school grounds—a concrete tennis-court, a patch of lawn just big enough for some restricted games, a swimming-pool and a ball-alley—felt vast, especially if for any reason you had to traverse them during school hours when they were empty and silent. In my first year this happened once a day as I made my way up from 1st to 2nd class for Irish. Ballinatone NS had done its work sufficiently well that I was thought too advanced for Irish with the rest of the 1st class.

However, whatever reputation I had for academic attainment in one subject or another was soon matched by my notoriety as a 'difficult' pupil. I was always in trouble. My clothes were never right, my hair would never sit down. I can remember being stopped by a teacher midway through one day's school who asked why I was wearing only one sock: I had been unable to find the other one under my bed. I got absorbed in reading a book and didn't realize the bell had gone. I talked back to teachers. I had terrible, uncontrollable temper tantrums. I refused to eat up my food.

It is hard to imagine anyone actually liking boarding-school food, but by comparing notes with what was served in my wife Eleanor's English school, I can honestly claim that we were not very well fed. Breakfast six days a week was primarily porridge—lumpy, thin or burned, as the case might be. Only on Sunday did we see the luxury of cornflakes and a fry—and Sunday was a torture because you couldn't get up until 8.15 instead of the usual 7.15, and had that much longer to wait for anything to eat. (I have always been an early riser.) Dinner was the main meal of the day: meat of some description, Irish stew being for me the ultimate horror, followed by pudding. Tea at 5.30 brought baked beans, sliced white bread, margarine and jam always served in unlimited quantities, it has to be said. And late at night some very stale left-over bread and a steel jug of watery milk was put out for anyone sufficiently ravenous to need it for supper.

The rows for me came with the requirement that you should eat up what was put on your plate. You could request a small helping but that small helping you had to eat, for the good of your character if not for the nourishment of your body. There was one showdown in which I was forced to sit at table long into the afternoon over the cold remains of some especially noxious bread-and-butter pudding.

I cannot now remember whether my nerve broke: I believe I may have forced down a spoonful, though I won false credit for holding out to the end. My parents were much bewildered some time later when summoned to a meeting with the headmaster to be consulted on my 'problems'. 'Now we know he cannot eat eggs', began Mr Brockhouse. My parents, thinking of the two fried eggs I could wolf down for breakfast at home, nodded uncertainly. It seems that the ingredient in the bread-and-butter pudding to which I had gestured with gagging nausea was egg.

On reflection, in retrospect, I realized that I must have been miserable more or less my whole time in Drogheda. But because of the advance publicity from Rufus about how wonderful it was and my excited anticipation of going there, I never told myself I was miserable. I didn't have real friends; at best there was one other boy who shared my strange habit of reading books. We were both so low in the school pecking-order as to become associates by default. I was small and uncouth, always infatuated with one girl or another, who was completely unaware of my existence. I flew into rages in which I kicked and screamed and yelled, but then suffered agonies of shame afterwards. I spent the last two terms of my school career sleeping in the corridor, banished from my dormitory for some forgotten misdemeanour. I could find no way of adjusting to the environment or to the system around me.

It wasn't that I was an outsider, different from the other kids at the school. It is true that many of the children came from small farming or shopkeeping families, their time in Drogheda up to the age of sixteen being all the education their parents envisaged for them. But there was a fair mix also of pupils from abroad: some Icelanders and Dutch, a sprinkling of English who had failed the Eleven Plus or who had parents who worked abroad. (It was from one of them, Kerry Scott, that I first heard of Kuwait, or Q8 as I imagined it to be.) Only once was my Jewishness mentioned. I had scored high in some Maths test and Mr Pope had remarked that this must be my Jewish blood coming out. One of my fellow pupils was indignant on my behalf after class. 'What a thing to say—to accuse you of being Jewish!' My father being a professor was used to account for my being 'brainy', but it wasn't really any sort of stigma, nor yet distinction.

I was miserable at DGS (without knowing that I was) for all the standard boarding-school reasons: I was homesick, I felt I didn't fit in, I was unpopular, I was cold, I was hungry, my hair stuck up, my father visited me in yellow American workman's boots. There was running through it all the sick feeling of impotence and incompetence, the inability to get a grip on things either inside or out. The only consolation of school, and that a partial one, was playing games.

CHAPTER TWELVE

Hockey

Drogheda Minor Cup Hockey Team, with J.R. Pope on left, Leonard Horan on right. I am third from the right in back row

Mr Horan must have had a first name but, as with most of the teachers, we didn't know what it was. I christened him Biffo and the name stuck. He was large and athletic and had a voluminous moustache frothing over his upper lip. It was said that he would have been selected to throw the hammer for Ireland in the 1940 Olympics if the 1940 Olympics had happened. As it was, he was left teaching Irish and games. He was the sort of big man who had no means of imposing himself on others except by his size and strength and we all, secure in our Quaker immunity from corporal punishment, knew he could not touch us; the days of beating around the head with Latin dictionaries was over. So his classes were one long, ineffective bluster. Mr Horan insisted on everyone standing up when he entered the room, as a mark of discipline: 'Class up, Grene out', became his routine bark as I, rising from my desk with a studied and insolent slowness, was sent to stand outside the classroom door by way of punishment. My National School Irish, which had me starting well above the Drogheda standard, soon slipped back, what with the generally half-hearted way the school taught it under Catholic state compulsion and my frequent enforced absences from Biffo's instruction in the language.

The irony was that, while I was top of Biffo's blacklist in Irish, the first disruptive suspect to be sent out of class, I could nearly always regain his favour on the games field. Because at games I was exemplary. Not that I was especially gifted athletically: I had poor co-ordination and no ball sense. But I was willing to run my heart out on a games pitch. I always liked running itself, I liked being part of a team, I was prepared to compete to compensate for my lack of natural ability. And so by sheer effort—and the tiny size of the school—I could find myself Drogheda Grammar School Intermediate Athletics Champion and captain of the Minor Cup Team in hockey.

The boys as well as the girls playing hockey was a feature of Drogheda as a Protestant co-ed school. We never aspired to rugby, or only half-heartedly towards the end of my time at Drogheda, when we were beaten by some horrendous margin by the under-12 boys of Headfort prep school. The one taste I had of serious rugby later in Belfast had me moving to cross-country running within a matter of weeks. No way did I want to submit myself to the fierce physical mauling involved in that relentless contact sport; I might have been competitive, but not that competitive.

With hockey it was different. Again there was the prior inspiration of Rufus. There had been the mysterious beauty of the sprung wooden hockey stick with its elegant curl at the end, so genteelly superior to the rough wooden hurls I had occasionally handled belonging to the Clash hurling team. And then there was the ritual of wrapping the lower end of the stick with white insulation tape to reduce the sting up through your hands when you hit the hard white ball. Rufus was full of the excitements of hockey, very like me as eager team competitor, and I was enthused by her enthusiasm.

We trained in a games pitch some distance out of the town which had the added interest of the cement-factory buckets crossing it on their own special elevated railway. Drogheda was, for Ireland in the 1950s, a fairly industrialized centre. There was the port, with huge heaps of pink gypsum from Kingscourt in County Cavan heaped on the quays, ideal for sliding down if you weren't too fussy about your clothes. There was the Stork Margarine factory and, inseparable from it in our minds, the oil and cake mills. And dominating Drogheda out on its northern edge was the cement factory, with a properly factory amount of chimneys, smoke and dust. Even though school outings were often organized to the factories and I am sure we all had plenty of opportunities to learn the details of the manufacture of cement, none of us quite knew what travelled in the heavy metal cars that trundled along the wires above our heads from pylon to pylon. There were always dares to climb one of the pylons and be carried along in one of the buckets; there were even fantasies of sending the hockey ball soaring up into one of them, thus putting an end to the game for the day. For the most part, they remained the always present, largely unnoticed, speechless overhead monitors of our games.

I cannot imagine why I liked hockey so much, given that I played it so badly. I couldn't hit the ball straight, I couldn't pass accurately, I couldn't dribble—that all-important skill of keeping the ball tapping along and under your control while you ran down the pitch avoiding the opponents who tried to tackle you. But I could sometimes spoil the play of those opponents when they had the ball by pursuing them, worrying them, refusing to give up. So I was placed as one of the half-backs, the first line of defence against the opposition attack. For a time, as captain of the Minor Cup Team—to play for the Minor

Cup you had to be under fourteen and Drogheda probably only just about had eleven boys under fourteen to make up such a team—I was given the crucial pivotal role of centre-back. But with the advent of a new boy quite evidently better at hockey than I was, I was moved sideways to right half-back, though I continued to have the honour of (capt.) after my name when the team was set out in traditional 5:3:2:1 formation. It must have looked very odd for teams from other schools. The captain nearly always played at centre-forward, the key striker, or at centre-back, the key defender. And it wasn't as though I had special leadership skills on the pitch. It was just that I didn't give up, didn't accept I was beaten even when it was clear to everyone else. Which is, I suppose, a leadership skill of a sort.

The treat of playing hockey was to go on an away game, almost always to Dublin. Dundalk Grammar School, our all but twin just twenty miles farther north, didn't play hockey, and we never travelled north of the Border. It was to King's Hospital that we went, or to Mountjoy, Avoca, Kingstown, a cluster of Protestant secondary schools, very few of which were to survive past the 1960s in unamalgamated, unreconstructed form. They almost always beat us. To be fair, some of them were all boys, so that even if they, like us, had small numbers, they were likely to have twice as many eligible hockey players to choose from. Once, I can remember we managed the pinnacle of success of reaching the quarter-finals of the Minor Cup. We played against Avoca, I think it was. I recall all too vividly the beautifully level playing field—our games pitch seemed always to revert to grazing land in the summer—and the immaculately clear white lines. I remember also repeatedly failing to centre the ball, failing to hit it— doing everything possible wrong, so that it seemed like my very own personal humiliation when we were (expectedly) beaten.

It was the extra special teas laid on at the away schools that provided consolation for the usual bruising defeat. And there was the trip back to look forward to. Amiens Street Station was nothing new to most of us, though it did have the wonderful red machine where for a moderate investment you could turn the stiff hand in succession to the several letters of your name and produce in embossed aluminium NICHOLAS GRENE to proclaim your identity on anything worth identifying as yours. The stations out from Dublin were all too familiar, the familiar tedium particularly of the slow trains stopping at Raheny, Killester, Donabate, Skerries, Bettystown and Laytown before finally making it into Drogheda and the twenty-minute walk from the station to the school.

But a precious half-hour loose in O'Connell Street—that was really the pay-off of the away game outings. There were the would-be glitzy, would be American cafés like Cafollas; there was Britain's excuse for a hamburger chain, Wimpy's—all to us the height of metropolitan chic. Above all, right under Nelson's Pillar, there was the lure of the Amusements Arcade. It was here that I learned my vulnerability to the addiction of gambling, a lesson in retrospect I suppose cheaply earned, though it seemed anything but cheap at the time. Not for us the fruit-machines that required the insertion of a whole sixpence each time, a sixpence swallowed remorselessly each time two lemons appeared in conjunction with a strawberry. Instead, there was a brilliant game much better adjusted to school pocket-money budgets where you could roll a halfpenny on to a moving cloth and hope to land it on the stripes that returned your halfpenny doubled, trebled or even sextupled.

I hazarded whatever halfpennies I had in my pocket, watched the pig and its bonhams on each one roll unproductively into the maw of the machine. Once or twice I may have got a couple back, enough to fire me on to roll again. I was hooked enough when I came to the end of my coins to go up to the money-changing booth and come away with ten shillings in halfpennies. I have no idea how I came to have a ten-shilling note in the first place, that bright orange-red picture of Lady Lavery, only just less large and extravagant-feeling than the same lady in green. Our weekly pocket money, dispensed by the school from a reserve deposited by our parents, was a uniform ninepence. But I did have the secret resource of a Post Office Savings Book, into which birthday and Christmas presents were deposited—those lovely pink slips in dollars from Edith Neisser and my grandfather—and I may have dug deeper than usual into this fund in anticipation of our outing to Dublin.

There is a scene in *War and Peace* where Nicholas Rostov gambles at cards with the villainous Dolokhov until he has lost 43,000 roubles: Dolokhov fixes in advance the number of thousands he is going to take off Nicholas by calculating the sum of the ages of himself and Sonia, the girl he loves hopelessly and who worships Nicholas. It is one of those horribly painful scenes that Tolstoy does so well in all its feverish unreality. But for me the pain is cued to the memory of seeing ten shillings in halfpennies, no less than 240 coins, go wheeling away in the Amusements Arcade in O'Connell Street! I learned my lesson: I have never gambled since, never been tempted to gamble.

Summer brought an end to the hockey season and, in compensation, came the loveliest time in Drogheda. For a start, the summer term was short. Depending on when Easter fell, it might not begin until the last weeks of April and it was over by 30 June. (We had heard with horror from English school friends of terms that went on until late July.) This was very different from the long 15-week trudge from September to Christmas, or the black days of January and February when Easter seemed merely a mirage. School in its spring greenery looked visibly nice even to the disenchanted eyes of those constantly immured there. There were rows of ornamental cherry-trees at the top and bottom of the lawn where we did the sort of sports that needed only limited space. I have an action shot of myself crossing the bar of a high jump in amazingly unclassic style. To sit beneath the trees in full pink bloom was to feel a whiff at least of the grace of spring. Tennis and athletics in white aertex shirts and shorts took the place of the muddied trials of the hockey pitch.

There was one summer when the zeal of a good resolution led me to go out at the first bell (7.15 a.m.), run a couple of rounds

Crossing the bar, with the fine Drogheda Grammar School building (now destroyed) in the background

of the 'track', the cinder path skirting the school grounds, and end up with a swim in the minuscule outdoor swimming-pool. It gave me a glow of virtue for the rest of the day. As a lifelong routine-junkie, school, the most routine-bound of lives, should have suited me well. For the most part, however, the set timetables of school were burdensome to me; not because they were set timetables and restricted me from some longed-for individual freedom but because they involved repeated actions I disliked in themselves: school meals, classes where I was always in one sort of trouble or another, enforced Sunday afternoon walks where I was cold and bored. But give me a routine I set myself, out of bed each morning the minute the bell went, into my running things, racing round the track in the cool morning air or even in the rain, and then splashing about in the swimming-pool with its light skim of cherry-blossom, towelling down afterwards—and I was happy. That was as happy as it got for me at Drogheda Grammar School.

CHAPTER THIRTEEN

Illness and Divorce

At school in Drogheda around 1960

My father used to keep a large hard-bound brown account book in which he reckoned up retrospectively the outgoings and income of the farm in preparation for the income tax return, which was largely a work of fiction. For years after he sold the whole sheep flock, they kept dying off in twos and threes as far as the Revenue Commissioners were concerned: otherwise, a large one-off payment for their sale would have been due. The accounts for the year 1959 were headed 'Year of my illness'.

My father had always suffered from duodenal ulcers, as had his father before him. I can remember being told about my grandfather having a bad haemorrhage one day and my then twelve-year-old father being sent by his mother to fetch a doctor—no telephone in the Belmont Avenue house in those days. My own memories of earlier crises in my father's health were largely based on hearsay. There was the time he haemorrhaged on the farm in Lemont and was dashed by ambulance into Chicago, the ambulance men heard to say on looking in at him, still to the good when they arrived: 'Sometimes we get them there, sometimes we don't.' That was when my mother, never having driven before, had to make her maiden voyage along Garfield Boulevard, with impatient drivers behind her rolling down their windows and shouting, 'Lady, get a horse'. There had been one episode in Ireland when my father had been hospitalized and treated by the surgeon Victor Synge; I can recall his commenting on the surgeon's relationship to the playwright. But 1959 was different.

Home from school at Easter, I knew my father was in pain. We used to play draughts in the evening—I never did get very far with chess—and he usually beat me. I was triumphant one night that I had managed to overcome him with some special double jump, taking out two of his kings at once. Then looking up into his face, I was ashamed of my gloating; the grey face of my opponent showed only too clearly that he was not really able to concentrate on the game.

I was at school when he was taken into hospital in Dublin and was only told that he had undergone a major operation, its scale being registered by the fact that it lasted six and a quarter hours. I was taken to see him just once, a few days after the operation, in a nursing home on Pembroke Street. He lay there looking sleepy and dazed, and I couldn't find anything to say to him. He apparently told my mother that I shouldn't be brought in again because the sight had shocked me too much. In fact, the shock came later when

I came back to Clash and saw him in the aftermath of the operation.

My father had always been a heavy man, some fourteen stone, definitely overweight for someone of his build. He paid absolutely no attention to dietary recommendations for his health at any stage of his life. Heavy drinking, cigarettes, high fat, no fruit or vegetables: you lived the way you wanted to live, not according to some absurd doctor's fads. The very idea of drinking milk for his ulcers had him in fits of rage: a dairy farmer who gave much of his life to producing the substance, who loved milking above almost any other human activity, he loathed the taste of the stuff. I can remember the look of fascinated horror that came over his face as he watched my young half-brothers Andrew and Gregory gulp down quarts of milk. In his seventies, after he had undergone surgery for colon cancer, I once mildly suggested that he might reduce his salt intake. He rounded on me, pointed out that he had lived to be a septuagenarian heaping salt on his food, and he wasn't about to stop.

In June 1959 the fourteen-stone father I was used to was suddenly before me as a skeletal wraith of himself, having lost over six stone. It was a frail and fretful old man who sat up in the bed of the downstairs sickroom where he remained, unable to manage the stairs. I had no idea just what continued to be wrong with him, but I was only too aware of the smells that came from the bag into which a tube from his side drained. I don't think I ever consciously framed the thought that he was going to die. But that face, with the bone structure surfacing from beneath the familiar, sanguine, fleshed-out countenance, remains for me the image of imminent death.

He hung on in that state all summer. He often told a story evocative of the time and of the character of our friend Tom Cullen. My father was fond of Tom and enjoyed his company, even though he never worked closely with him, as I was to do later. At one point, in the desperation of his continuing illness, when nothing he ate seemed digestible, my father had a mad craving for hare; a hare stew would be just the thing to set him up again, and Tom would be the man to find the animal for him. The days went by and there was no sign of the longed-for hare. At last, on one of Tom's visits to the sickroom, my father raised the matter with him: 'Tom, did you ever manage to get that hare you promised me?' Tom looked guilt-stricken. 'I did not, Mr Grene, I'll tell you the truth. I knew where there was one to be got, in your own Top Fields, and I took the gun with me. And sure enough, there he was, a big jack-hare sitting up. And I looked at him, Mr Grene, and you know, I hadn't the heart to kill him.'

My father was not a 'good' invalid, to say the least. It's possible that it is only bad invalids who survive, invalids with the energy and determination to resist the will of their doctors and nurses and insist on their own recovery. But it certainly makes life difficult for those around. The man who thought that the rich gamey meat of a hare would be ideal for a convalescent after extensive intestinal surgery also thought that outings in the pony and trap would do him good. He had recently bought an unusual four-wheeled gig—not the normal so-called roundabout trap on two wheels where the passengers sat sideways to the shafts in a high-sided, semi-rounded carriage. This was a two-seater among traps, with a single bench squarely set up behind the pony and minimal protective sides.

To this vehicle my little Ginger was harnessed and my father and I set out together on a round trip that was to take us up the Whaley Abbey road with our farm on both sides, round down the Whaley Abbey avenue and out on to the main Aughrim Road home. I had driven a pony and trap quite a lot. On one disastrous occasion when driving with Lil Corrigan, I scraped the side of a neighbour's van, with expensive consequences. It cost £20 to repair the—to me—extremely minor scratches I had left on Mr Fletcher's van. But on the whole I was regarded as a trustworthy driver, so I was given the reins when my father and I set out in our natty little four-wheeled gig. All went well until we were on our homeward journey on the Aughrim Road. On a stretch where there is a quite steep downward slope, the trap with its four wheels, which was probably a little too big for the diminutive Ginger in any case, started to run up on her. Driven on by the trap, she started to bolt. I couldn't hold her—I never could hold her when she took it into her head to run away. My father tried to take the reins from me but, weakened as he was, he could not hold her either. And a milk lorry could be seen coming up the road just a couple of bends away. As the best chance we had, my father pulled the reins sharply to the right and drove Ginger into the grassy ditch, the left-hand side being a blank stone wall. The trap overturned and my father and I were thrown out on the road.

I have no distinct memory of what happened after that. The milk lorry must have stopped; passers-by came to the rescue. My immediate terror was that my father might have been killed, and that it was my fault. Miraculously, however, even in his enfeebled state pitched out on to the tarmac, he was no more than badly shaken. I acquired a cut on my upper lip from the abrasion of the road surface that turned into another permanent scar, another body mark of my lifestory along with the sickle-cut from my childhood in Illinois. At the end of the summer, my father boarded the plane for Chicago looking more dead than alive, and returned the following year fully recovered. He never regained his full fourteen stone weight, and was no doubt the fitter for it.

It was two years after this time of illness that everything changed permanently. One summer day, my father and I were taking Ginger over to Tullow to breed her to an Arab stallion there. On a straight stretch of road just past Aughrim, he turned to me and said: 'Marjorie and I are going to get a divorce. You must have realized that we have been unhappy for years'. I had never realized anything of the sort. There had always been rows, screaming-matches over this and that, but how was I to know that was 'unhappy'? You only have your own parents and the way they behave is the way parents behave. At thirteen I had no classification for a good or a bad marriage. And to someone brought up as I had been in rural County Wicklow, divorce seemed unimaginable. Divorcées were women in books with scarlet-painted fingernails. This was the more absurd because I had met American friends of my parents who were divorced, like the much-married Maurice Donoghue. But such transatlantic polygamy was an exoticism of over there, something of a joke; it couldn't happen here.

Still, it *was* happening here. And as my father continued to talk, explaining how he and Ethel had long been in love, a whole lot of things that hadn't made sense before were suddenly explained. There were the recent absences of my father, day-trips away from Clash to distant parts of the country which had no avowed purpose. He had been looking at other farms he might buy to live in with Ethel, including the one in Belturbet he eventually bought. Further back than that, other memories returned to mind, newly transfigured by understanding. Ethel Weiss, always known to us as Esh, had originally been a student of my father's and had been Rufus's babysitter. Rufus had been especially attached to her, and she stayed in touch with both of us when we moved to Ireland, sending presents to us each Christmas. At this moment on the road to Tinahely, I recalled, with retrospectively cringing vividness, pressing my mother to admire a riding-crop that Esh had sent me and being puzzled at her cool response. I registered now also other hangnails that had snagged against my normal assumptions about my parents. My father was a great admirer of the Stuart kings and I had been wondering with my mother at his devotion to Charles II. 'He identifies with him', my mother had said', 'he thinks like the king, acts like the king'. 'But not when it comes to Charles's promiscuity', I replied with all the complacent priggishness of my years. 'Hmm' was all my mother said.

I was deeply, horribly upset by my parents' parting, but for all the wrong reasons. If I was honest with myself, I wasn't really sorry my father was leaving home. I pretended to care about that because I knew it was expected. In fact, at thirteen, I rather looked forward to the idea of becoming the man about the place, to taking charge of the farm. My father was an enormous presence, warm, loving and vehement; he didn't leave much room for the sense of independent personhood. The terrible trauma of divorce for me was the social shame it represented. For the one year I remained at Drogheda after my father left home, it was a secret I revealed to no one. When the smug, hated headmaster Mr Brockhouse (who presumably had been informed by my parents) ventured some well-intentioned words of sympathy, I hated him all the more for it. Only much later on in my time at school in Belfast did I finally confide in one of my closest friends that my parents were divorced. The image of the scarlet-painted fingernails remained with me throughout.

CHAPTER FOURTEEN

Crossing the Border

My mother, Senior Lecturer in Philosophy, Queen's University Belfast

In Drogheda Grammar School there was a little corridor leading from the dormitory block into the playground. On a broad ledge below a window in this corridor, post was laid out once a day and a scrum of kids formed, eager to see was there anything for them. Once every couple of weeks, there was an envelope for me with distinctive American stamps, and even more distinctively, my address typed way up in the left-hand corner. My father's letters, often several sheets folded very small and scrunched into the envelope, were long and leisurely, responses to my last budget of news, descriptions of his teaching in Chicago, or of the fall colours as he rode in the Forest Preserve, the vast natural park not far from the city which he loved so much. I recall in particular one letter in which he decried the merits of J.D. Salinger—I had clearly written under the overwhelming impact of my first reading of *The Catcher in the Rye*—and recommending to me instead a novelist who had just joined the Committee on Social Thought. I can remember being struck by the oddity of the titles of his books—*Henderson the Rain King*, *Seize the Day*, *Dangling Man*—but thought it might just be my father's partisanship that made him so enthusiastic. It wasn't until *Herzog* became a bestseller that I actually read Saul Bellow and could get student street cred from having signed copies of his works.

My mother's letters were much shorter but more frequent and their stamps bore the young Queen Elizabeth's head on them with the little ribbons sticking out behind. From the time I went away to school, my mother had been working in Britain. To begin with, she had been part-time research assistant with the scientist turned philosopher Michael Polanyi at the University of Manchester. At one point she had taught extra-mural courses for the Workers' Educational Association in Lancashire. Then she got a job for a year at the University of Leeds, as a researcher in the Department of Education, visiting schools all over Yorkshire to investigate the teaching of biology. A domestic upheaval, a member of the Philosophy Department running away with another colleague's wife, created a vacancy that allowed my mother, at last, after a gap of some fifteen years, to regain a position as a university lecturer in philosophy.

The letters from my mother were always welcome, and all the more welcome for their occasional enclosures. In 1950s' Ireland there was still protection for home industries, including confectionery. As a result, the staple sweets of the neighbouring island—Mars Bars, Milky Ways and the like—were contraband exotica unavailable to the deprived children of the Republic. We had to make do with the evidently inferior Irish counterparts: instead of the Mars Bar, in all its sticky, chewy, creamy luxuriousness, there was a Big Five with shamelessly similar wrapping, but hard, tasteless and textureless by comparison. A Mars Bar would not have been fitted into a standard envelope, might have been confiscated by the Customs. But flat Yo-Yo biscuits or Wagon Wheels could be slipped inside the sheets of the Leeds letters. They arrived somewhat battered, broken and crumby inside their wrappers; they were no less delicious for that. There was an added relish to reading my mother's often scribbled notes with Yo-Yo biscuit crumbs still adhering to them.

I had one half-term holiday with my mother in England when she was based in Leeds. It was my first experience of travelling alone on the Irish ferry to Liverpool, my first glimpse of Britain. My anxious mother booked me a first-class cabin on the B+I from the North Wall; I have the impression of the grandeur of a solo cabin and linen sheets, something radically unlike any other subsequent crossings of the Irish Sea. She was there to meet me at Liverpool, where I was briefly disappointed by buses that were green and not red. Still the steam-powered train that we took across the Pennines to Leeds was suitably different from the diesel engines already introduced in Ireland. We travelled on to York where I duly admired the gleaming white bulk of the Minster, before crossing back across England to spend the rest of the weekend with friends of my mother who lived near Chester. The echoing spaces of the huge railway station, flying smuts in the wind, unimaginably continuous miles of houses and more houses, the medieval streets of York, the red-brick walls of Chester, all this made up the otherness of England.

A new job for my mother brought me into contact with another otherness. In 1960 she was appointed to a lecturership in Queen's University Belfast. It must have been the following St Patrick's Day that I first made the trip north to a part of the island quite as distant in our Southern imaginations as Britain itself. There were a substantial number of pupils from Northern Ireland in Drogheda; places like Belfast, Lisburn, Newtownards were familiar to us as the home addresses of school friends. They were privileged people with easy access to the sweets we were denied, including Spangles, glamorous fruit-drops that seemed a particular specialty of the North. And yet, though we had occasionally crossed the high viaduct over the Boyne on our way to Dundalk, the journey beyond that forbidding barrier, the Border, appeared unimaginable.

The St Patrick's Day trip was a bit of a letdown. A train took me to Belfast through places with unfamiliar-sounding names like Portadown. But then with only a momentary stay in my mother's flat on the Stranmillis Road, we had to set out on the return journey by car back to Drogheda. It was exciting to drive through the Mountains of Mourne (if only because of Percy French), to puzzle over bizarre place-names like Loughbrickland, to discover that Northern Ireland was an extended countryside of farms and farmland, not just the city of Belfast. Still, I can hardly say that my first venture across the Border was a revelation. Like Keats's naughty boy, I found that the ground was as hard, that a yard was as long … as in the Republic of Ireland.

My father's leaving, my parents' divorce, brought altered prospects. My mother, liberated from my father's likes and dislikes, set about changing her life. A new upstairs bathroom was installed in Clash, so that the trek down through the kitchen to the freezing facilities below was no longer necessary. A fridge was bought, now that my father's disapproval of all refrigerated food was no longer a household law. And, most significantly of all, my mother was able to buy her first ever new car, a Mini of the sort that had just begun to roll in their hundreds of thousands off the British assembly lines of Austin/Morris. My father always regarded investment in new cars as a hideous waste of money; only in his mid-eighties, coming into an unexpected windfall, did he finally buy a non-pre-owned vehicle, a modest Toyota. Used as he was to huge, heavy American machines, he specially disliked the flimsy family sardine-cans that dominated the British market. So to buy a Mini, the diminutive box built around just four people, and to buy it new ex-works, was to signal as markedly as possible my mother's new status as *femme sole*. She was deeply hurt by my father's departure, grieved over it for half her lifetime to come, but at least she could drive a smart new Mini.

She could also take her fourteen-year-old son out of boarding-school and bring him to live with her in Belfast. It had always been planned that I would follow my sister's lead and leave Drogheda after the Intermediate Certificate. Whatever my parents' reasons for sending us to Drogheda in the first place, they had no illusions about its academic standards. We would have to go somewhere else to be prepared for entrance to university. With the change in our family situation, it made more sense for me to move to Belfast, where I could live with my mother and go to a local day-school rather than attend a Dublin school and have to board with a Dublin family as Rufus had. So it was decided that from September 1962, Belfast would be my new home, Belfast Royal Academy my new school.

Sitting the Inter was thus to be the end of my ten years' schooling in the Republic. DGS did not have enough pupils taking the exam for it to be a separate exam centre, so we had to bicycle out to a local convent in Greenhills, some miles out of Drogheda, for our exams. I arrived each day equipped with a bar of chocolate, which I duly consumed halfway through the morning exam to provide me with an energy boost to get me through the next hour and a half's writing.

The day of the Irish exam was different. All through my time at Drogheda, my National School Irish, quite strong when I first arrived, had steadily declined, as I became ever more disaffected. There was no support from home: neither of my parents knew any Irish and resented its compulsory status as a state stupidity. The teaching at Drogheda was poor, the Protestant school doing not much more than going through the motions of instructing us in the allegedly first national language. Still, we had all be prepared to sit the Honours level in Irish, drilled through the set poems— 'Droimfhionn Donn Dílis', Pearse's 'Bean tSleibhe ag Caoineadh a Mhic', Máire Mac an tSaoi's 'An Chéad Bhróg'.

At the exam, I was determined to revolt. I had done the mutinous minimum of preparation for it, learning off by heart a few of the set-piece synopses of the prescribed poems, practising the essays that always began 'I well remember…' But I needed to mark my rejection of Irish more dramatically than that. So when the exam question papers were being distributed, I boldly raised my hand for the Pass level instead of the Honours. An absurd gesture, but some sort of public rejection of Irish and all it stood for as a meaningless school imposition.

That wasn't the end of my anti-Irish dramatization. Conscious that my Irish studies were over, that in Belfast Royal Academy Irish would not even be available, much less required as a school subject, I determined to celebrate my freedom. I don't suppose I realized at the time the political significance of my chosen site, but it was to be on the green grassy slopes of the Boyne that I brought my Irish books, notes, practice essays and *bunábhar*s for mass incineration. I have never destroyed a book before or since; my mother used to horrify me by her willingness to throw away thrillers she had read. It seems like a point of principle that anything in print should be preserved: someone, somewhere might want to read it. Yet, on that June day by the Boyne, I watched with vicious pleasure the pages of my Irish poetry anthology curl in the flames, turning from white to yellow to brown to crumbling black ash. I was ready to cross the Border.

CHAPTER FIFTEEN

High-towered Academy

Belfast Royal Academy on Cliftonville Road

Some perverse principle seems always to ensure that parents, anxious to do the educational best for their children, end up sending them to schools as inconveniently far away as possible. Drogheda was a long seventy miles away from Clash by road when there were no by-passes and no way of avoiding Dublin. The best my parents could manage when they took me out from school for the day was lunch in Dublin Airport—where there was a very upmarket restaurant with a luxurious sweet-trolley that I can still remember—or a visit to the zoo. By the end of the day, whatever old banger they were driving would have covered something like 200 miles.

For the day-schools in Belfast, the distances were different but the maximum inconvenience principle continued to operate. We lived on the southern side of the city close to Queen's University, initially right round the corner in Fitzroy Avenue, in a house rented from a colleague of my mother's who was on sabbatical, then in a little semi-detached in Stranmillis. I could have gone to Methodist College at the bottom of the Malone Road, walkable from where we lived. I could have gone to Inst, the Royal Belfast Academical Institution, as famous for its literary alumni (Michael Longley and Derek Mahon among them) as for its rugby: Inst was downtown, an easy bus ride away. But, no, I went instead to Belfast Royal Academy, BRA, so confusingly close to the RBAI initials of Inst—BRA that was to hell and gone up on the north side of the city off the Cliftonville Road. That meant either two buses, one into town and another out again the other side, or the crosstown 77 that made its way across both the Falls Road and the Shankill, a route that apparently had to be discontinued during the Troubles when such bi-sectarian peregrinations became impossible. And it was that 77 bus I took every day, a 45-minute journey with additional walks at either end.

I don't remember who recommended BRA to my mother—I think a colleague at Queen's whose wife taught there. Methody was thought to be too big, Inst was all boys and my parents had always favoured co-education. So it was BRA for me. And it was a good school, where I was well taught, even if it laboured under something of a sense of inferiority relative to its better-known Belfast rivals. Our school song that saluted 'High-towered Academy, great B R A' had an air of compensatory overstatement to it.

My first impression of the school, coming up for interview and assessment when I was still in my last term at Drogheda, was less of its high towers (though these were impressive enough in their Victorian way) as of the sheer numbers of boys and girls who crowded its corridors and staircases. Drogheda under the headmastership of Mr Brockhouse had moved up from an enrolment of sixty to a hundred, but I was quite unprepared for the jostling, pushing, yelling mass of humanity represented by BRA's 1,000 pupils moving from class to class. That in itself was something new to me. In Drogheda you sat in your own desk in your own classroom right through the school day, and the different subject teachers came to you. Here, at the end of each forty minutes, an immense scrum of boys and girls aged eleven to eighteen shoved their way as best they could from class to class.

BRA was a direct-grant grammar school, funded by the state but with the right to take private pupils. There were, in fact, very few of the latter, the great majority were north Belfast children from the neighbourhood, selected by the academic Eleven Plus exam system. The school prided itself on 'setting' rather than 'streaming', that is dividing pupils into subject-specific groups according to ability, instead of placing them into a single higher or lower class. This was what necessitated the constant changes in classroom, as a boy in Class 2A for Maths might have to make his way to Class 2D for English. Timetabling, in an era before computers, must have been a nightmare.

On that first day when I visited the school, I was moved, shell-shocked, through the uniformed masses now to one teacher, now to another, to assess which set I should be in for each subject. However, when I made it up to Belfast in September 1962, somehow my assessment sheet had got mislaid and I was stuck into more or less random sets: 4C for English, 4F for Maths, 4A for Physics and Chemistry. My quite respectable results of the Intermediate exam came through eventually—BRA was not to know the dishonourable significance of my Pass Irish—and some of my classes were changed. I was shot up from 4F to 4A for Maths, but it proved impossible for me to be moved from 4C for English. So, for a whole year of my schooling I kept company with the cream of Maths and Science students, while sticking with the middle-of-the-roaders in my best subject.

It was no doubt good for me. If I spent two and a half hours a night labouring over my simultaneous equations or calculus, I came out about even with the kids who had whipped through their homework in ten minutes. In Science it was less beneficial. At the end of a year studying light and sound, my teacher charitably said I might have made a reasonable Physics student. But I was the despair of my very patient Chemistry instructor. When he had worked through the principles of valency point by point for a whole hour and at last asked, 'Now, is that clear?', I raised a bemused hand: 'Just forget it, Grene', he said resignedly, at that stage knowing I had no future in Chemistry.

In the humanities, meanwhile, I was thriving. After years of being drilled through James Carty's *Class-book of Irish History*, the prescribed text with its patriotic nationalist narrative, it was a pleasure to get my teeth into the 1832 Reform Bill, the details of nineteenth-century British social legislation. History and current politics were not kept in separate compartments either. We had a passionately left-wing history teacher, who exultantly predicted the coming of a Labour government and the ending of the long dark years of Tory rule.

The school itself felt very alien at first. There were not only all those bodies in uniform dark blue and purple. Drogheda had a uniform, but only for state occasions; in BRA you would never dare to appear without the regulation school-crested blazer, grey flannel trousers, school cap and tie. There was also the bewildering anarchy of breaks and lunch-time with these thousand adolescents released to mill about the concrete expanse of playground. We were segregated by sex, boys on one side of the school, girls on the other, with a tuck-shop tucked in between where all those long sought-after Mars Bars and Milky Ways could be freely purchased.

By degrees, you came to locate little knots of familiar faces that hung around in one particular part of the playground. In my first year I identified myself with the good boys, the diligent bespectacled students earnestly committed to their studies. I can remember a deal struck with one such in which he was to give me lessons in German (which he took and I didn't) in exchange for lessons in Greek (one of my electives). We did play an occasional game of tip-rugby with a rolled-up cap for a ball, but for the most part breaks were spent in self-consciously self-improving conversation.

Every now and then, somewhere on the playground, a cry would go up of 'Fight, fight, fight!' Suddenly the swarm of milling male bodies would gather around the combatants. The fights rarely lasted long—a schoolmaster on duty would come running to break it up—but I was appalled by what felt like the unrestrained ferocity of the fight while it lasted and the blood-hungry enthusiasm of the onlookers. This was *Tom Brown's Schooldays*, Belfast-style.

Belfast Royal Academy was Protestant, of course, solidly and exclusively Protestant. The school itself would not have excluded a Catholic pupil, if one had applied. Years after my time, when the Foster family moved to Belfast, young Brian was sent there: it was the school of which Alec had once been headmaster. But Northern Ireland was a rigidly segregated society in matters such as education, and the sectarian selectiveness of the system was not something the schools had to enforce. On the 77 bus, one was conscious of it when the BRA school cap elicited jeers of 'Wee Prod' from other kids on the bus in the Falls Road area. Otherwise, shuttling between the educated enclave of my mother's Queen's colleagues and my Protestant schoolfellows, religion was not an issue for me.

It was there, of course, in the city. The structure of the school year ensured that I was always safely off in Wicklow on the 12th of July. But shortly after I arrived in Belfast, the fiftieth anniversary of the 1912 Solemn League and Covenant was celebrated with fitting fervour and I had a chance to see Orange loyalism on the march. I remember the Divis Street riots which, in the light of the terrible events of the 1970s and 1980s, seem a fairly minor eruption of the violence that was to come. At the time, though, burned-out buses not far from where the 77 trundled along seemed quite alarming enough.

Strange as it seemed at first, I soon became acculturated in the special society of 'high-towered Academy'. As my midwestern accent had been rapidly replaced by thick country Wicklow in 1952, so by Christmas 1962 I was coming to mimic the upward-ending intonations of my BRA friends, their distinctive vocabulary of 'wee's and 'whenever's. For the first time in my educational career I was fitting in, coming to be something like a model student. (My mother was surprised—I myself was astonished—when they made me a prefect in my final year at school.) I moved on from my goody-goody group of friends to a small band of self-styled intellectual oddballs.

The nucleus of this was the Greek class, all three of us. There was John Millar, nicknamed 'Moenia' (Latin for city walls) for his solid build; there was S.T.P. (Singy for Singleton) Wilson, who adorned all his exercise-books with drawings of armoured Greek hoplites; and there was me. I had done a very little Greek with Mr Pope in Drogheda, but because it wasn't part of the school curriculum it had to be in lessons outside class privately paid for by my parents, which both Mr Pope and I managed for the most part to skip. Now for the first time, I had proper classes and got beyond the *First Steps in Greek* with its wonderful sentences for translation: 'They are driving the wagons into the sea', 'It is difficult to persuade lions'. Our teacher, Mr Clarke, arguing that no one knew what classical Greek sounded like, taught us to pronounce it as if it were modern Greek, which made us sound bizarre to conventional classicists.

But then bizarre was what we wanted to be anyway. To do Greek at all singled you out as unusual, and we prided ourselves on our dissident elite status. Our group included also some non-Greeks of similar tastes and temperament: Richard Gray, clever, cynical, debonair, with something of the air of the hard man about him; Michael Faulkner—Catholic, but English Catholic, which made all the difference—a St John's Ambulance volunteer giving him the enviable right on volunteering days to appear in black and white St John's gear instead of regular school uniform; nice, gentle Robert

Lobb, who lived quite close to the school where we could all go together and listen to the Rolling Stones. (Poor Robert: not normally profane, he was overheard by his mother one day exclaiming 'Oh fuck!' 'Some day, Robert', she told him in sadly reproving tones, 'you'll learn the meaning of that word and you'll be very sorry!')

We fancied ourselves as the literate intellectuals. We read the *New Statesman* like the concerned left-wingers we took ourselves to be; we would gather each Monday to talk over the *Observer* book reviews. My own affectation of highbrow tastes went as far as listening to the BBC Third Programme, trying to understand Schoenberg, going to the opera when (very occasionally) such a thing was to be had at the Belfast Opera House. To my everlasting regret, I did not queue with others in my class—almost all girls—to go to the Beatles concert when they played in Belfast. I cannot always have been tuning in to the Third, however, because I do remember hearing the Beatles' first single 'Love Me Do' on the radio, and going through Lime Street on a school trip to Paris, when 'She Loves You' had really put Liverpool on the map. 'Did you ever see anything grander in your lives?' asked our French teacher rhetorically as we stood at the Arc de Triomphe looking down the Champs Elysées: 'Royal Avenue on a Saturday night, sir', came the untraceable riposte from the back of the group.

Our little clique played up to our school reputation for difference by giving off the airs of a gay coterie, and singing loudly scurrilous songs. As far as I know, we were all straight and it was well before the time when any schoolboys would have officially come out: I was astonished to find such a thing happening in my children's schools a generation later. I was certainly extremely innocent in all matters sexual, still confining my romantic inclinations to unavowed passions for one girl or another in my class. But I sang along lustily with the obscene parodies that were devised by my wittier and more knowing friends.

Because I lived on the south side of the city, so far from the rest of my friends, I was very bored for much of my Belfast years. For the only time in my life, I watched long hours of mind-numbing television. I remember dreary walks by the Lagan not far from our house on a Sunday, those Sundays when famously even the swings in the children's playgrounds were locked out of sabbatarian zeal. I have hated Sundays in cities ever since. I was spoiled rotten by my mother, who catered to my every need, even to the extent of leaving supplies of beer in the house when she went away so I could invite my friends over from far-off north Belfast. They had never heard of such a mother. No doubt, I was moody in typical teenage fashion, certainly nothing like grateful enough for the pampered life she enabled me to lead. Still, it was a good time for me, finding like-minded friends, doing school work that on the whole I enjoyed, with teachers who (given the inevitable exceptions) I could respect, not being subjected to the privations of boarding school. I have always felt grateful to Belfast and Belfast people ever since.

CHAPTER SIXTEEN

Derrycark

Derrycark farmhouse, Belturbet, Co. Cavan

My remarried father had found a new farm for himself and Ethel near Belturbet in County Cavan, a much smaller farm than Clash, just forty-five acres of boggy land beside a lake in drumlin country. Derrycark was some eighty miles south of Belfast and my father used to come up for the day to visit me, as he had visited me in Drogheda. We would meet at a hotel near the City Hall and go out to walk in the countryside. Our game was to walk through fields of bullocks and try to guess their weight; priding himself at his ability in this, he was always the arbiter of how close I had come. Eventually late in the afternoon, we would join Ethel, who had spent the hours we were out bullock-weight-watching in a hotel on the outskirts of the city, and we would have tea together. Inevitably there came a tussle over when and for how long I was to be allowed to visit my father and Ethel in their new

Cavan home. My mother did not want me to go there at all; my sister at first loyally refused to go, though she did visit eventually. But I was too cowardly to stand up to my father's emotional appeals, and in spite of my mother's evident unhappiness agreed to spend a week of my summer holidays at Derrycark.

It was farming very unlike anything I had seen before. All the farms on the Derrycark road were small like my father's, indeed many of them much smaller: when he bought it, one neighbour remarked that he was getting a 'big ranch of a place'. Everyone kept a few cows and shipped milk to the creamery. There was something I initially heard as the 'core' and only afterwards recognized as '*comhar*', Irish for help—a sharing of labour and equipment that only made sense with so many tiny farming units. It was the only community I had ever seen in Ireland where it wasn't immediately evident who was Catholic and who was Protestant. In Wicklow the tiny minority of Protestants were readily identifiable. In Belfast the communities kept well apart from one another. But in rural Cavan, right on the Border, where the population was split about evenly between the two religions, there seemed to be an easy tolerance and a spirit of relaxed co-operation between people of different faiths. That was to change markedly with the onset of the Troubles, when Catholics and Protestants continued to work together and be civil to one another, but with large silent areas of reserve that had to be walked round.

This part of Ireland appeared to a stranger like myself also to be without that social stratification I was used to in Wicklow, where the landless labourers (or unemployed) of the cottages were regarded as well beneath the small farmers who looked up grudgingly to the big tillage men. No doubt there were unseen class distinctions in Belturbet too, but it appeared as if the small size of all the landholdings, the fact that there were no workmen, all the work being done by family members, made for a relative equality of status. In spite of spending only half the year there, in spite of their superior education and off-farm income, my father and Ethel tried strenuously to fit in along with the other small farming families. I took it that it was at Ethel's insistence that the neighbours called them by their first names: it was startling to hear my father called David rather then the ubiquitous Wicklow Mr Grene. The people who worked with them—small, wiry, bespectacled Sonny Emery, or large, laughing Willie Magee—came as friends and neighbours, not as hired hands. David and Ethel took pains to be accepted and in some sort succeeded. When the time came for them to return to Chicago each autumn, the farm left in the charge of a neighbour for the winter months, a party was thrown in the local Lawn Hotel where large numbers of neighbours came to join in a community celebration. In a modified form, now held at the Derrycark house, the annual Grene party survives to this day.

I hadn't seen a farming community like this before, but I hadn't seen land like that either. The Wicklow farm was on the slopes of the hills, the soil was light and easy-draining; however much it rained, a day and and a half and it was more or less dry again. Not so in Cavan. With impermeable limestone underneath, the heavy clay on top held every single drop of rain—and that was a considerable number. Statistically, no doubt other parts of Ireland get more rain than Cavan, but it didn't feel like that. The tiny fields sheltered by gigantic blackthorn hedges that threatened to engulf them did not help. Every hoofprint of cow or horse remained in place and filled up with water. The gaps from field to field became mudholes in which the proverbial ass and cart could drown. A famous story was told in Eleanor's family of a visit to Derrycark by Hubert and Peggy Butler, in which one of Hubert's wellingtons became irrecoverably sucked into the mud. 'Can you imagine, my dear?' Peggy would say, 'each year they go from Chicago to *that*!' They did indeed, and seemed to love it.

My father was always an improving farmer. He never believed in imposing a textbook model of farming regardless of local conditions; he always said you had to look around your neighbourhood, observe best practice and try to follow it, with improvements if possible. So he early accepted that tillage was impossible in Cavan conditions. It had to remain the most permanent of permanent pasture. But he set about putting down drains and removing some of the more unnecessary of the cancerous *sceach* hedges. The trouble with taking out the hedges was working out what to do with the enormous resulting spoil, the vast piles of roots and thorns which sat around on the fields, blighting growth below them. And the flattened mud left behind where the hedges had been removed took years, it seemed, before they would grow anything. The drainage no doubt helped the productivity of the farm long-term. But I remember being led by my incurably optimistic father into a space that looked like Flanders with bullrushes and being invited to admire what a change the drains had produced. 'Can't you see the difference, Nicky?' I would be asked. 'Er, yes', I would reply with a gulp.

Haymaking under such conditions was a major ordeal. John McGahern's novels and short stories, set in neighbouring Leitrim/Roscommon, vividly evoke the drama of saving the hay. The long sequence in *Amongst Women* catches brilliantly the sense of urgency, the need for titanic effort on the part of everyone, if (for once) the sun was shining. But McGahern vastly foreshortens the process so that it appears to happen in not much more than two days. Unless Leitrim was very unlike Cavan, it rarely was accomplished under a week, even if the weather favoured you, which of course it rarely did. I can recall having to lift wisps of hay off the water-filled potholes of the meadow in an effort to dry it.

It was very labour-intensive, even more than in Wicklow, and required help from the neighbours if, unlike so many of the local people, you did not have a family of six or seven children. The hay had to be handled repeatedly—literally handled in the initial stages. Old Mr Ferguson, our next-door neighbour with his piercing blue eyes, would walk along with bent back, reaching down to wrap the hay around his arms into 'laps', circular hay-doughnuts that sat up off the ground so air could go through them. Then if rain threatened, the laps were turned into hobblers, mini-cocks that would save it, at least partially, from the wet. These had then to be shaken out again to re-dry before at last being put up into proper cocks. It was not work that my father enjoyed: the slow laboriousness, the endless frustrations and delays, the gloom of seeing the rain come down in the evening, destroying the day's work. When it became possible to make big baled silage wrapped in black plastic, it was with vehement satisfaction that my father declared that he would never try to save hay again.

It was the daily routine of milking that he really enjoyed. I liked it too, if it hadn't started so early in the morning and gone on so long without sustenance. At 6.30 or before, a knock would be heard at my door: 'Nicky, Nicky, are you awake?' I stumbled sleepily from my bed and dragged on my clothes. I have inherited from my mother the need to breakfast first thing before being capable of meeting the day; my father would have none of such effete practices. We went out to set about the two- to three-hour business of feeding the animals, milking, and getting ready the churns to go off to the

My father milking at Derrycark

creamery in Belturbet. That was the second half of the morning ordeal. The churns were loaded into the pony-trap and my father, Ethel and myself squashed in around them and set off the two miles to Belturbet.

At that stage still, there would often be a line half a mile long of tractors and trailers, horse-carts and ass-carts all queuing to get up to the creamery intake. Our trap inched its way forward until, at last, we would be in sight of the amazing frothing, foaming, open stainless-steel tank of milk into which our churns would be emptied, though not before the hawk-eyed creamery manager, Paddy Reilly, scooped a sample to check its butter-fat content. Then there were the messages to do in the town before returning to the farm: collecting animal-feed or fertilizer, stopping by the newsagent for the specially ordered *Irish Times*—only the *Independent* would have normally been for sale. A date for one such trip is supplied by my memory of Ethel opening the paper and exclaiming that Marilyn Monroe had died. Finally, at last, at long last, we would be back in Derrycark, and the horse unyoked from the shafts of the trap, there was breakfast. It was a huge breakfast, a gargantuan breakfast of eggs, bacon, sausages, kidneys, heaps of toast and bottomless cups of tea, and coming at one o'clock just about saving me from what felt like imminent death by starvation.

I got on well with Ethel. I liked the profusion of poultry that animated the farmyard, splashing ducks and hissing geese, an old horse-box come to rest in one corner tenanted by baby chicks under an infra-red light, transported from the incubator that Ethel had installed in the central upstairs bedroom of the house. The house itself sat just across the road from the yard, looking out over the farm to the lake. It was much newer than our house in Clash, built in the 1940s, but it hadn't been lived in for some years when the Grenes acquired it in 1962. Their style of living was spartan to say the least, the house subordinated to the needs of the farm: there was (of course) no central heating and, until the prospect of a visit from

Ethel's Chicago city mother some six years after they had moved in, no curtains. Creature comforts were not high on their list of priorities. They had no telephone and continued without one for many years, on the plausible-seeming grounds that they had all too much of the telephone back in Chicago. All urgent communications to them had to go by telegram.

The lack of creature comforts—delayed breakfast apart—did not especially bother me. Such uneasiness as I felt in my visits to Derrycark had to do with my anomalous position in the household, at once a visitor and a member of the family. Ethel used to introduce me as 'a son of David's', which sounded vaguely Biblical to me. I suspected that she hesitated to use the word 'stepson' out of reluctance to claim even a step-maternal role for herself. But as no word of explanation was made as to my mother or my father's first marriage, I seemed as if dropped from the sky, a fully grown fourteen-year-old son of David. No doubt this was largely my own self-consciousness, and people would have been well capable of working out for themselves who I was. Still it meant that, for all my enjoyment of my visits to Derrycark—the novelty of the surroundings, the interest of the life there, the pleasure of my father and Ethel's company—I always returned home to Wicklow at the end of my week's stay with a sense of strain relieved.

CHAPTER SEVENTEEN

Israel and France

Watertower at Kibbutz Negba, damaged in 1948 war, retained as monument

Rufus's boyfriend Pete Alscher came from New York. We had been rather surprised when he became her boyfriend, though we had known him for years. As a poor lost lad of sixteen, who had for some unaccountable reason taken it into his head to do Philosophy at Trinity, he had been invited down to Clash for his first Christmas in Ireland, and then for all subsequent Christmases. He was fun, with a zany sense of humour, and he gave me my first serious books as a Christmas present—the books he cared about: *A Portrait of the Artist*, *The Catcher in the Rye*, *Decline and Fall*. I could not bear the Waugh, the comedy much too black for my fourteen-year-old self, but I was overwhelmed by the other two: Stephen Dedalus and Holden Caulfield were wonderfully different role models of adolescent rebellion. Pete was in Clash as Rufus's friend, not boyfriend. For much of her time as a Natural Sciences student in Trinity she had been involved passionately, and in the end unhappily, with someone else. So the change in Pete's status in her final year took us aback, though we were happy for both of them, liking Pete as we did.

Pete's family—his high-school teacher mother Ruth, younger brother Colin and sister Jan—had moved to Israel to work on a kibbutz for a year which then turned into two. I am not sure whose idea it was that I should visit them for a few weeks in the summer. Anyway, after an abortive attempt to find funding for the trip—I flew to London for an interview with some young Jewish association only to be told that I had to be eighteen to be eligible—my ever generous mother decided to pay for it all herself. And aged sixteen, in the summer of 1964, I was off to do that most fashionable of 1960s things to do in the summer: work on a kibbutz.

It should have been a dream journey, and in part it was. I flew from Belfast to Paris and then boarded a train that would take me overnight to Venice. Eating *crêpes aux fruits de mer* in a dining-car with linen tablecloths and gleaming cutlery as we sped across France was my absolute high point of high living up to that date. Of Venice I remember little: I was bussed from the train station to the docks where I was to board the *Theodor Herzl* of the Israeli Zim Lines.

This is where things began to get uneasy for me. My mother was Jewish: that made me Jewish too, according to the matrilinear principles of Judaism. But her family were well on the liberal side of Reformed; she once told me that 'kosher' was regarded as a dirty word in her household. I had grown up with a Protestant National

School familiarity with the Scriptures, including all those Old Testament kings and prophets. Of Jewish customs, traditions and history I was innocent. I had therefore no idea who Theodor Herzl was. And I could not imagine why people looked so scandalized on the boat when I asked for white instead of black coffee. Nobody had ever told me that you couldn't have milk dishes and meat dishes in the same meal. (At least I hadn't told any of my fellow passengers about that delicious seafood pancake on the train.) I felt an imposter, a fraud, whose ignorant Gentile ways would have me expelled from the kibbutz the first day I arrived.

In the event, I need not have worried: the first day I spent on the kibbutz, we were served ham for lunch. Kibbutz Negba, on the edge of the Negev desert as its name implied, was a completely secular left-wing institution affiliated to the Israeli Labour Party, no kin to the right-wing religious kibbutzim that also existed, many of them much richer and better resourced than Negba. The rearing of pigs had actually been banned in Israel the year before I arrived, but some continued to be produced by means of a splendidly ingenious technicality. They were kept on raised platforms, and therefore not on the holy ground of Israel itself.

The Alschers had come up from the kibbutz to meet me in Haifa, and a sore and sad me it was they met on the quay as the boat docked. I had run through the pleasures of the *Theodor Herzl* within twenty-four hours of leaving Venice, had visited all the decks available to economy passengers of my class, had tried out all the amusements and settled down to be bored. A half-day stop in Greece allowed me just time to make it up to the Parthenon and have it to say that I had stood on the Acropolis, but the event that should have been a landmark moment of the trip for a classics student like myself left shamingly little impression beyond a great deal of broken marble and a certain number of ruined walls and pillars. One was conscious that the ship also had numbers of other passengers: Romanian immigrants to Israel who travelled in the 1964 equivalent of steerage without the benefit of the multiple decks, the swimming-pool and the games; and posh first-class people who lounged on more comfortable deckchairs at their own exclusive poolside.

We did have our pool, too, as midships economy passengers. And on the last afternoon before we were due to reach Haifa, I sat down to read beside it in my T-shirt and shorts and fell asleep. I can only have snoozed there for an hour or an hour and a half, but with my fair skin and complete innocence of sunscreen, the consequences were deadly. By evening my shoulders and legs had gone from a suspicious pink to an appalling livid red. The last night in my bunk was murderous. Any contact at all with sheet or blanket was a sting-ray touch; sleep was out of the question. So it was that dazed, only half-awake and sun-broiled, I first set foot in Asia. I dimly remember a train trip from Haifa to Tel Aviv, a day spent trailing around what struck me as a most unprepossessing city before taking the bus south to Ashkelon. 'Tell it not in Gath, proclaim it not in the streets of Askelon', I repeated to myself, without remembering what it was I was not to proclaim. It did seem extraordinary to be taking something as mundane and modern as a bus to this Old Testament place.

Kibbutz Negba, when we finally reached it by jeep, was a scatter of buildings and a patchwork of cultivated fields and orchards emerging out of the surrounding sand and scrub. I was often told its history by some of its founding members: how the land had been bought by them when they arrived as immigrants in the 1930s, how they worked on the roads to pay off the debt, tilling the land early in the morning or late at night. I was shown with pride the shot-scarred old water-tower that stood as monument to the 1948 war when the kibbutz had held out for six weeks against attacking Egyptian forces. Everything had then to be rebuilt from scratch. The resulting chauvinism (original sense) of the kibbutzniks was understandable; I was expected to admire their democratic organization, in which all adult members had an equal share in the running of the kibbutz, their support for the education of their young people at university at home in Israel or abroad, the industry and application with which they had made the desert bloom. If at times your powers of admiration seemed taxed to their limit—'Really, your cows on the kibbutz have four legs each, that is remarkable!'—you felt they had earned the right to boast.

I was given a bed in a room in the part of the kibbutz assigned to adolescents. Sadly for me, it was in a room with two other boys. I had heard with sixteen-year-old excitement that the rooms were not sexually segregated and had been enormously looking forward to sharing space with someone female for the first time in my life. In fact, many of the dormitories were mixed; it just so happened that mine wasn't—just my luck. I dare say the kibbutz equivalent of incest taboo ensured that the boys and girls in shared rooms did not have sex. My ambitions were hardly that daring anyway: I looked forward to nothing more than furtive glimpses of unclothed girls' bodies. Instead I had to make do with two grumpy and silent boys, getting up and dressing with me at 4.30 in the morning.

For that was when the jeep called to take us out to the fields to start work. Given the temperatures from midday on, you worked from 5 until 11.30, then went back home to sleep through the scorching afternoons. Unlike my father's wake-up call in Derrycark at 6.30, it was good to be out at dawn in the pear-orchards, being assigned your bag and stepladder and heading off to pick the fruit. The trees were unexpectedly small but just high enough so you couldn't pick from the ground. The pears were rock-hard; whether they would be artificially ripened later I had no idea. My job was to climb the ladder, fill the carrier that was slung round my neck, empty it into the waiting tractor and trailer and come back for another fill. I had always thought I liked picking fruit but in Negba I learned the difference between the thrill of hunting for apples or raspberries in your own garden—with the prospect of eating a fair proportion of what you picked—and the wearisomely repetitive business of a commercial operation. Still, the break from work came within a couple of hours, with refreshments to be had under the shade of the trees, and by 11.30 or so you were back in the dining-room for lunch and free for the rest of the day.

The ham I had been served on my first Israeli Sabbath turned out to have been a one-off. Meat was in fact rarely served. Coming from a heavily carnivorous family, I found it strange at first to be given a do-it-yourself meal of raw vegetables—cucumbers, peppers, tomatoes—to be made into a salad according to your own tastes, with the occasional egg for protein. The revelation was the yoghurt. I had in fact met yoghurt before when Rufus brought back from a visit to Paris an aluminium yoghurt-maker with its own octagonal glass containers. Gleaming, exotic and magical it all looked, but I couldn't be persuaded to eat the stuff. Here in Negba, though, hungry after my morning's work, with options limited, I tucked in to any one of the three, four or five different types of yoghurt on offer: thicker or thinner, smoother or more textured, unbelievably delicious with coils of golden honey dripped over its white surface.

I had tried to prepare for my visit to the kibbutz by teaching myself Hebrew: *Teach Yourself Hebrew* was the name of the book I had bought in Mullans on Royal Avenue in Belfast. I just about managed to learn the letters, to get over the fact that there were only consonants, the vowels being indicated (if at all) by dots above or below the characters. But the sentences I painstakingly spelled out were not, I guessed, going to prove especially useful where I was going: 'The priest was right in the sight of the Lord'. I more or less gave up. The only real advantage I gained from my efforts was the ability to scrawl *aleph*, *beth* or *ghimel* on the crates of apples when I was one day assigned the job of sorting them into A, B or third-class G categories. The result of my Hebrewless state was that I was incapable of communicating with the others in my age-group. They apparently referred to me as 'the dumb one', or 'the white one', for my pinko-grey skin refused to turn anything darker than a flushed red.

I thus had no interaction with my peers, at least not with the genuine kibbutzniks, the children of the elected members of the kibbutz. The kibbutz was indeed a democratic collective, as claimed, but full membership was not easy to gain. If you weren't the child of members, you had to work for a considerable length of time to be eligible for election. But in the adolescent enclave, as well as such birthright kibbutzniks, there were kids whose parents were not members—Romanian or Russian emigrants who lived in Ashkelon but who boarded out their children in the kibbutz where they could get a superior education and, maybe one day, the chance of joining the outfit. With these lads, who were in Negba on sufferance, I did talk, even though their English was often not much more advanced than my Hebrew; within the limits of our linguistic competence, we became friends. The true Negba-ites, no doubt fed up with occasional birds of passage like myself, stayed sullen and silent, even though (I was told) they actually could speak fluent English if they wished.

I would have been very lonely if it hadn't been for the Alschers, but then they were the reason I had come. I got on extremely well with Colin, who was just my age, and who inducted me into the gag-lines of American comedy shows that seemed to me hilarious, even though I had no idea where they came from: 'I accept the allegation, but I rejects the allegator'. I laughed because he laughed. Jan was sufficiently younger than Colin for me to disregard her, following his big brotherly lead. But I hugely enjoyed my evening visits to Ruth's small house in the grown-up part of the kibbutz. Ruth was large, warm and refreshingly vulgar, the daughter of Russian Jewish immigrants who had taken a career break from her teaching job to experience Israel at first hand. (I was to meet her extraordinary mother later in New York: a little old lady keeping a hatshop in New York, like something out of Bernard Malamud, still after a lifetime in the US unable to speak anything much except Russian and Yiddish.) Ruth mothered me, laughed at me and with me, gave me wise advice that I always remembered and never followed—'If you whine and complain to people about being ill, you have to be prepared to do what they tell you to get better'. The Alschers represented an alternative Jewish-American culture that was to me quite foreign but to which, because of my mother, I could somehow technically lay claim. Trying to adapt to their family ways I thought of as a piece of exciting but implausible impersonation.

Israel in 1964 was still a secular state where the Labour Party was the natural party of government. This was before the June war of 1967, before the Yom Kippur war of 1973, before the occupation of large swathes of neighbouring territory and the aggressive policy of West Bank settlement. When I was there, the hot political issue was that of the Bene Israel, a group of immigrants from India who claimed Jewish descent but whose Jewish credentials were being called into question by the authorities: the Israeli Rabbinate was eventually to declare them 'full Jews'. It was a revelation to me to discover how Asian a country Israel in fact was at that stage: two-thirds of the population were Asian rather than European or American Jews. And the kibbutzim, which seemed the feature of the state of Israel that everyone had heard about, were home to a tiny 2 per cent of the population, though I was told proudly they produced 10 per cent of the country's food.

With Negba's 1948 history, it was inevitable that the people I talked to—the adults who, unlike their teenage children, *were* willing to talk to me—should see their own position and that of Israel as a whole as a community under siege. I was told about how at the very point of the setting up of the state, they were attacked simultaneously by their four Arab neighbours. Well, perhaps it was true that there were Palestinian refugees in camps in Gaza, but that was only because they were kept there by Egypt for propaganda purposes. Israel had never done anything except try to defend itself from the much larger countries on their borders whose avowed purpose was to drive all Jews into the sea. I could see even at the time that this was only one side of the story, open to challenge from the unvoiced other side. But the experience of having been in Israel, of being exposed to such feelings and attitudes has left me politically torn on the subject ever since. When most of my friends and family are passionately, unreservedly pro-Palestinian, outraged at the outrageous policies of the Israeli government and the brutality of the Israeli Defence Forces, I can understand their indignation, but have a wriggling residue of another view: how is a state, set up under such circumstances, likely to respond to a phalanx of neighbouring countries dedicated to its annihilation? No justification for what has been done, for the settlements policy, the appalling building of the wall bisecting the Palestinian territory, the aggression against the Lebanon and the Gaza strip: still, you have got to see where it is all coming from, which the conventionally anti-Israeli line does not.

I was in Israel during the summer of 1964; the following summer I spent in France. I had given up French halfway through my A-level year to make more time for Latin and Greek, but still hoped to learn to speak it more fluently than could be achieved by drilling in vocabulary and irregular verbs. Years before, when she was still at school, my sister had been au pair with a French family in Normandy—my mother and I had visited her; and, though Rufus hated most of that experience, it had improved her fluency in French. I couldn't really imagine what one did as a male au pair where there were no children to look after but I duly headed off to *la famille* Turpault in Maine et Loire, and I soon found out.

The Turpaults had a small farm not far from Cholet, a town apparently only known for its handkerchiefs: if I mentioned it to French people subsequently the universal response was 'Ah, les mouchoirs de Cholet'. M. Turpault must have had some other occupation—I never found out what—but had retired to his inherited country house to farm in a quiet way. It was large for a farmhouse but definitely too small for a château, tall and shuttered, as I remember it. Monsieur was mild-mannered, thin and bespectacled with pink cheeks; Madame looked like one's idea of a short, solid, middle-aged bourgeoise. One daughter remained at home—others were married and lived elsewhere—the frail-looking Aline, who seemed always anxious to pre-empt the domestic criticism that regularly came her way. I can remember one lunch-time entirely spent in remonstrations on her having chosen a Camembert that was not ripe enough. There was also a son, Henri, lumpish and loutish to my disenchanted eyes. He was the youngest of the family, almost exactly my age and had just taken his *baccalauréat*, as I had just taken my A-levels. However, I was definitely not 'au pair' with him, in that he did nothing discernible except mug up the French Rules of the Road for the written exam required in order to get his *permis de conduire*, while I laboured in the fields.

I arrived at a weekend and was initially given nothing to do, except help Henri roll the lawn tennis court. I can remember thinking how bored I would be, if I never got to work on the farm. Some bitter recollection that. For from the Monday morning I started on what was to be the daily routine: breakfast by myself at 7.30—I was shown where the coffee and milk were left out ready to heat up on the stove, and I could help myself to the *pain de campagne* that was delivered to the house three times a week. Then it was on to the day's work, beginning with the feeding of the rabbits. This was my pleasantest task, poking in greenery to the doe rabbits with their young, watching the half-grown black and white bunnies scamper around in the hay when I came in to deliver their concentrates. From time to time there would be one less of the more fully developed rabbits to be found, and that evening we would have delicious *civet de lapin* for supper. And when I finished with my rabbit-feeding duties, I indulged myself with smoking a pipe, my seventeen-year-old affectation of the time.

But then came the real work of the day. I was given no part in the milking of the herd of Jersey cows: that was done by the regular workman Michel and his wife, who had a pretty cottage in the farmyard, and completed probably long before I got up. My main job, it soon transpired, was to *enlever les mauvaises herbes*; it seemed a strangely roundabout way to describe what in English is the one-word verb to 'weed'. At first I was set simply to get rid of the nettles that grew around the farmyard, but after that it was out to the fields of beet where drill after unending drill had to be weeded. And at that I worked a normal workman's hours, from 8.30 to 6.00 with the respectably French hour and a half off for lunch. I did occasionally learn some agricultural phrases; I can still remember that what we call the PTO of the tractor—the power take-off—is *la prise de force*. But I wasn't going to get fluent communing with the sugar beet. And mealtime conversations among the Turpaults were to me so dull that there seemed little incentive to get involved. If one lunch was devoted to the iniquities of Aline in the selection of a Camembert *pas assez bien fait*, others were given over to the rival merits of different sorts of roofing or the best boots to wear when out shooting. No doubt interesting issues for the Turpaults, but hardly riveting for a seventeen-year-old Irish boy.

It turned out that I was only one in a steady succession of unwaged Anglophone au pairs. That was the explanation for Henri's surprising fluency in English swearwords, and for the English newspapers I had found lying about my attic bedroom when I arrived, left behind by the previous occupant who had departed the previous day. He sounded as if he had had more initiative than I, and had found his way to the pubs of Cholet from time to time. I only lurked and sulked around the place grumbling to myself. Michel was some consolation when I got to work with him because he was a fellow dissident, as disgruntled with his employers as I was. Early in my time *chez* Turpault, there was the excitement of the harvest—a full two months before we would have been cutting grain in Ireland. It gave me my first and only experience of poaching, when a pheasant, driven out of the wheat, was cornered in a ditch and dispatched by Michel with a dung-fork, as I guarded the one possible hole by which he could escape. I was sworn to secrecy—M. Turpault, a sportsman, would have been incensed had he known one of his pheasants had been slain in this barbarous way out of season—and I was rewarded with a share of the resulting casserole.

The few times I got to eat with Michel and his wife, when the Turpaults were away for a day, I learned what I took to be a lesson about French cuisine. If the dinner-time conversation was often mind-numbing, the food at the Turpault family table was good and I tucked in happily to seconds of rabbit. But I was surprised to discover that only Monsieur took wine with his dinner and then no more than a single glass of home-made rosé, whereas, at Michel's there was plenty of rough red wine and the food was a revelation. Though perhaps this was just because Michel's wife happened to be a very good cook, I got the impression that the pleasures of French cuisine grew from the bottom up: robust traditions of peasant cooking, people who had little money but used what they could grow, gather (or poach) resourcefully and inventively, filtered up into the more refined forms of the bourgeois kitchen.

A day spent with Michel also gave me my first real hangover. The Turpaults had gone off to a wedding; Michel decided this called for a holiday for the hands left alone on the farm. We spent the morning playing table-tennis—Henri was extremely surprised at how much my game had improved the next time I played with him. And in the afternoon Michel used the excuse of a long unreturned ladder borrowed from a neighbour for what turned into a protracted social call. We were asked to *boire un coup*, and one *coup* led to another. After several glasses of red wine, apricot brandy was served, a deceptively colourless liquid handed out in what seemed to be innocuously small quantities. The burn at the back of my throat as it went down was startling; the warm haze as I was rattled around in the empty tractor trailer returning home was agreeable enough. But the following morning, I had to announce to the family that I had a *crise* and would not be able to work that day. Great concern was shown, and I lolled in bed through the daylight hours conscious that the wages of sin were a delightful and unaccustomed idleness.

That bedroom was not fitted out for a life of leisure. There was a bed, a table, chair, and a wash handbasin with cold water: the only bathroom in the house adjoined the bedroom of M. and Mme Turpault where I was allowed to bath once a week. I was used to such deprivations from Drogheda Grammar School, even if the years of maternal pampering in Belfast had intervened. It was the lack of reading matter that bothered me most. For some impossibly high-minded reason, a zealous determination to educate myself perhaps, I had brought with me only the Bible and a translation of Plato's *Symposium*. I genuinely enjoyed the *Symposium* and made my way somewhat dutifully through the Gospels. But thereafter I was stuck. I ended up having to read the only book I found lying around, *Le General du Roi*, the French version of a novel by Daphne du Maurier in which the life of an appalling general of the English Civil War—I know just how appalling he was because I read up about him subsequently—was glamorized into a torrid historical romance. I suppose it was good for my French.

I am sure I could have made better use of my time in France, been less miserable, if I had been a small bit more adventurous or self-assertive. I know now what I didn't know then, the normal conditions for au pairs: time off to study the language, a reasonable weekly allowance of pocket money. As it was, I resented being used as unpaid labour force; I resented being introduced as *un jeune Anglais que nous avons à la maison*; I hated having to assist Michel in killing a calf and studiously refrained from eating the resulting veal—it ought to have turned me into a vegetarian but I was in the end much too greedy for that degree of moral principle. I got so fed up that I wrote to my father to send me a telegram demanding my immediate return home two weeks before the end of my agreed stay. M. Turpault grumbled that it was very inconvenient—he was clearly being left with a two-week gap before the next English-speaking weed-remover appeared. But he did, to my surprise, give me a fairly substantial lump sum on parting, so I did not go away empty-handed.

I left France with a souvenir packet of *les mouchoirs de Cholet*, an in-depth knowledge of the rival merits of *ardoises* and *tuiles* as roof coverings, and a rich vein in French obscenities lavished by Michel on General de Gaulle: no political animus there, just service in the army in Algeria where, he told me, he had not been paid. Does travel, as a late teenager, broaden the mind or merely extend the capacity for xenophobia?

CHAPTER EIGHTEEN

Going up to Trinity

Trinity College Dublin Front Square in the 1960s

It was always ordained that I would go to college in Trinity. Rufus had gone there four years before to read Natural Sciences, eventually specializing in Biochemistry: she would be due to leave as I arrived, without even the year's overlap we had at Drogheda. For my father, with memories of his glorious student career at Trinity, no other choice was conceivable. By way of parent-tease, I used to say that I would go to the Winnipeg Institute of Technology. Did such a place exist? I had no idea. If it did, it was far away and, as an institute of technology, was beyond imagination for my hidebound university-fixated father. A much more serious threat which I made occasionally was that I should go to University College Dublin. I had a long lecture from my father about the different ethos of the university he still referred to as 'National' and why Trinity was to be preferred. I have no idea how he would have felt if I had set myself to try to get in to Oxford or Cambridge: there would, I suspect, have been equally cogent reasons against them. But in any case I had no real doubt that I would eventually be following my father and my sister through that extraordinary Front Gate—that is if they let me in, something about which I was distinctly anxious. (I was rather huffed years later when a colleague of mine who had been to Queen's, at about the same time, remarked that it was a well-known fact among her Northern contemporaries that you could send a poodle dog up to Trinity.)

Whatever my parent-teasing remarks about the putative Winnipeg Institute of Technology or UCD, I did very badly want to go to Trinity. My father's reminiscences about his glory days in the 1930s were one thing, long ago history with which I could make little connection. But the life I saw my sister leading, the glimpses I had of her friends in Trinity when I was occasionally with her or when they came to visit us in Clash, had an intense, irresistible glamour. Though Rufus was a dedicated science student, committed from way back to being a scientist, many of her friends were in English, Modern Languages or Philosophy. Her closest friend and flat-mate was Nina Gilliam, daughter of Lawrence Gilliam the BBC producer, whose mother had married W.R. Rodgers the poet. Through Nina, Rufus met a whole range of literary people, including Brendan Kennelly, recently returned to Trinity as a lecturer, and Derek Mahon.

One afternoon in Dublin stands out above all in my memory. It was in the aftermath of Michael and Edna Longley's wedding and I was smuggled in to Jammets' back bar by Rufus. There a section of the wedding party had retired to sit out the 'holy hour' when all the ordinary pubs of Dublin were forced to close, but Jammets, because of its restaurant status, remained a refuge for the inveterately thirsty. There in a circle sat Derek, Brendan, a young and curly-haired Seamus Heaney and his lovely wife Marie. I can remember nothing of what was said, what I drank, how long it went on, nothing but the sensation of awe and delight at being admitted among the poets—all

Rufus with Pete Alscher and Derek Mahon

the Olympians. From then on, if I had had any uncertainty before, I knew that I wanted to go to Trinity, to be where these amazing people were to be found. The fact that I would have had a better chance of meeting the Longleys or the Heaneys back in Belfast never seemed to have occurred to me. To my prejudiced eyes, Dublin and Trinity were it; Belfast was the provincial backwater to be escaped. This was the propaganda I preached to my friends at school where the normal current of things took all university-going students to Queen's, with the occasional enterprising soul heading for Edinburgh or Glasgow. Trinity was intellectually cosomopolitan: why stay at home at stay-at-home old Queen's? This rhetoric even seemed to have worked with a couple of my friends who were to join me later at Trinity.

I was going to have to go somewhere in 1965 because there would no longer be a home for me in Belfast. My mother had moved to a lecturership in philosophy in Queen's in 1960 as part of the slow process of resuming her academic career. While still living on the farm in Clash, she had worked informally with Michael Polanyi in Manchester, helping him with research on his great book *Personal Knowledge*. She had held temporary positions at the University of Leeds from 1958 to 1960 when I was at boarding-school. But Queen's was the first regular job she had held since her contract had not been renewed at the University of Chicago in 1944.

My mother was glad enough to get it, though frustrated by the limitations on what she could do there. She was appointed to teach Greek philosophy, which proved a productive subject for her, resulting in her very successful book *A Portrait of Aristotle* (1963). (I can remember being amazed to discover long after that she had written the whole of that book in one year, while continuing to carry a full teaching load. When I exclaimed about this to her, she merely shrugged and said, 'There wasn't anything else to do'.) However, those were the days when *the* Professor of the subject laid down the curriculum and colleagues taught what he told them to—and in almost all cases it was indeed a 'he'. Bryce Gallie, my mother's boss, was a very witty, engaging political philosopher whose special interest was von Klausewitz. My mother and he got on well personally and she especially liked his ostentatiously outspoken wife, the Welsh novelist Menna Gallie. But Professor Gallie had no time for contemporary European philosophy nor yet the philosophy of science, my mother's special subjects; there was not even much opportunity for her to teach what she said she loved most, introductory history of philosophy. And so she began applying for jobs elsewhere.

She was shortlisted for a post in Cambridge; she narrowly missed becoming the inaugural Professor of Philosophy at the University of Lancaster, one of the batch of new universities being set up in Britain in the 1960s. Each interview brought new excitement with the prospect of a different sort of future, which we talked over together. At one point, when she thought she would have to stay permanently in Queen's, she considered buying a farm in Tyrone as an alternative to Clash. And then there came the advertisement for a professorship of philosophy at the University of California, Davis and this time there was no near miss. From some time in the autumn of 1964 it was clear that she would be moving back to America the following year, though all through that winter we waited for what she referred to as the 'gold-plated letter' that would confirm her appointment beyond doubt. It did arrive in due course and she was off to California. When congratulated by colleagues and friends on leaving the dank, grey climate of Belfast for the sunshine of the West Coast, my mother said that in fact the weather was the one thing she would miss in the move. 'I am glad to be going home', she said emphatically, 'to where I am allowed to teach the truth.'

I was in my Lower Sixth year at Belfast Royal Academy, the year when I was due to take my A-levels. There was a Middle Sixth for those who had to, or wanted to, repeat their A-levels, and an Upper Sixth for those who stayed on to take university entrance scholarship. The Lower Sixth was going to be the last year in Belfast for me, whatever happened. My father was bent on me taking the Trinity Entrance Scholarship, to him still with memories of 1930 *the* all important examination. Why not take it in the same year as A-levels, he asked? I was taken aback at doing something so outré. When we looked into it, it turned out that it wasn't going to be possible to take the Entrance exam in English (which I had already decided was going to be my degree subject) because it had a quite different syllabus from A-level English, but it might be feasible to do it in Classics, where all you had to do—all!—were unseen translations in Latin and Greek, no set books. So that was what I prepared to do, my A-level classes doubling with my Entrance

Scholarship preparation, with a bit of extra reading by myself. I can only remember reading Aristophanes' *The Frogs* on my own. Ploughed through with a Liddell and Scott lexicon beside me, word by obscene word, it didn't strike me as very funny. Though I did have a dream one night, in which I was having an argument with Euripides in what I took to be correct Attic Greek.

Because of this anomalous business of studying partly on my own, I gave myself license for a semi-independent policy by which I took Mondays off from school and went and hung out in the Belfast public library: I suppose I must have had the connivance of my mother to write excuse notes to take in each Tuesday. I felt terrifically liberated and grown-up swotting away through the hours of Monday, coming out each lunch-time to drink a half-pint of Guinness in a nearby pub. (Along with smoking a pipe, Guinness drinking was my other affectation of the time, though I couldn't convince myself enough of liking the taste to drink pints. At the end of the year, I decided that I didn't really enjoy either it or the pipe and gave them up together. Since then I have also proved a disappointment to foreign hosts where I am giving guest lectures as a specialist in Irish literature: I'm Irish, and I don't drink Guinness? what is this?)

It was an intimidating business, come May, to go up to Trinity to sit the Entrance Scholarship examination. You took it in the vast and glittering Exam Hall, where I was warned by my father that I was not to sit under the portrait of Queen Elizabeth—that brought bad luck. I felt I needed all the luck I could get sitting among those rows upon rows of little wooden desks and chairs with the raised dais in front of me and the towering organ-loft behind. Then, once the papers were opened and you began to write, you forgot your surroundings and worried only about what was the aorist of the verb 'to become'. However, I did glance up at one point during my Greek unseen and saw a very old man in an overcoat shuffling slowly across my line of vision. I bent back to wrestling with the knotty phrase on which I was stuck and looked up moments later to find he had disappeared. I checked one side of the hall and then the other: there was no door there. He had simply vanished into the panelling. I was convinced that all that dream-life of debating with Euripides had brought on brain fever: I was hallucinating, seeing things. I don't know when I eventually learned about the concealed doors set flush into the wood panels of the Exam Hall, or that the person I had seen was my father's old tutor in College, the philosopher Francis La Touche Godfrey. He belonged to the generation of Senior Fellows for whom there was no retirement age; he remained in his rooms in no. 1 Front Square where he had always resided. When it was raining as he came across from the Library, it was his habit to take a short cut through the Exam Hall, paying no attention whatsoever to any examination that might be in progress at the time. So like all those apparitions in eighteenth-century Gothic novels, my brain-fevered illusion of an elderly don materializing before my disturbed eyes had a solidly naturalistic explanation.

I did not think I had done very well in my examinations. I had a sticky oral with Professor W.B. Stanford, who wanted to know just why I was taking my entrance scholarship in Classics with the treacherous intention of reading English if I was admitted. 'Er, um, Professor Stanford, it's because it's easier…': perhaps not. I went over my unseens with my father who, though he tried to be encouraging, was clearly appalled at the howlers I had made. I was therefore thrilled and astonished when Rufus rang up from Dublin to say that I had got a Scholarship, in fact had placed fifth among the candidates. However, my puffed out chest was somewhat drawn in when I found out that two rivals from Inst, also taking Classics, were ahead of me. All my BRA inferiority complex was immediately reinstated. Still, in the autumn of 1965, I would be going up to Trinity.

CHAPTER NINETEEN

Freshman farmer

Border–Leicester sheep

Many students leave home in order to go to college; in my case, it was my family who left me in sole possession of our home. My mother had received her gold-plated letter, had shipped off her Belfast furniture to San Francisco by the Isthmus of Panama—'if you send it by the Isthmus it will never get there by Christmas, for the mail is oh so slow' she kept singing doubtfully to herself—and was installed in Davis, California. Rufus, with Pete Alscher, was heading to St Louis, Missouri, where they were both due to start graduate work in the autumn and, ahead of that, were immersing themselves in learning German in a tiny town called Achenmuhle. My father and his family, after the summer months on their farm in Cavan, in the annual rhythm of things would be off back to Chicago by October. I was to be the only one of the Grenes left in Ireland, and sole manager of the Clash farm.

For a year or so after my father left and my mother was working in Belfast, she tried to continue to run the farm at a distance, but it hadn't proved possible. Whatever the local help is like, you cannot operate a dairy farm by remote control, and in our case the local help was not great. So in 1963 the cows were sold, the land was let, and there were less urgent trips between Belfast and Wicklow. (The 140 miles down to Clash was a long trek, and I remember vividly the heavy snows of Christmas 1962 when the return journey involved walking up the ice-rutted, vehicle-impassible road through the village before first light, trying to make it to the train in Rathdrum.) I had been quite keen on working the farm in the immediate aftermath of my father's departure, but from the time I joined my mother in Fitzroy Avenue, I took no interest in it. Somehow or other, however, there had developed an idea that when I went to college, I would be given some money to buy stock of my own: a certain amount of the funds raised by the selling off of the dairy herd was set aside for that purpose. I think I may have stipulated this as a hazy Faustian pact with my own guilt at having switched off so completely from any farming involvement. So at the end of the summer of 1965, just before I started at Trinity, I was established in Clash with a farmhouse, a car, thirty Cheviot ewes and a Border-Leicester ram.

The sheep had been bought on my behalf by Tom Cullen with the £250 of my stock-buying fund. I was in fact still away in France when they were bought and they were already happily grazing in the Daisy Bank when I first laid eyes on them. The Border-Leicester ram was my father's idea; he was keen on the big frame of the lowland breed as a cross with the hardy Cheviot hill sheep that had been so thoroughly domesticated to the Wicklow mountains. In the event, the recognizable hooked Roman noses of the Border-Leicester proved a liability when we were trying to claim the state subsidy awarded only to pure Cheviot lambs, and those big frames actually made them hard to fatten on grass. The more closely set black-faced Suffolk ram, with his densely ridged creamier wool, was to turn out a better cross-breed. In the first excitement of animal ownership, I cared little for such nuances of genetic conformation: it was enough that they were there before me, all thirty-one of them, each with their four legs, their woolly bodies and their calmly uninterested eyes glancing up from grazing.

The car was a heavy black Hillman Minx, a respectably middle-class family car—in retrospect hardly particularly suitable for a novice farmer, and certainly no kin to the zoom zoom red two-seater that would have got my love-life as a young student off to a good start. I had learned to drive in my mother's Mini, rattling up and down the recently built M1 which at that stage went all of about five miles from Lisburn in the direction of Dublin before swerving off to Dungannon. It seems that it was a political impossibility in the early 1960s to plan a major road directed towards the capital of what Northerners, with studied anachronism, still called the Free State. The Hillman, when I acquired it, seemed like a sort of stately queen of the road, a Victoria among cars, after the tin-box-on-wheels Mini. After the best part of a summer driving illegally on my own with the provisional licence that demanded an accompanying qualified driver, I showed up at the Phoenix Park for my driving test. Sitting silent beside me, the test examiner instructed me to turn left and right round the by-ways of St James's Gate, put me through my paces of the three-point turn, before piloting me back to the test centre. After I had nervously answered the questions on the rules of the road he put to me, he said with a deadpan face: 'On this occasion, I regret to have to inform you that ... you have passed your test.' My licence went from provisional green to full red (it somehow seemed the wrong way round) and I could take to the wheel without worrying about being stopped by an inquisitive Garda.

I had a car, I had a farm, I had a house. I even had a washing-machine—the twin-tub for which Eleanor always claimed she married me—but I still didn't know where I was to live as a student in Dublin. In previous years Entrance Scholars had been entitled to rooms in Trinity, but already by 1965 pressure had mounted for the little accommodation available. There was nothing going for a fifth-placed Entrance Scholar, though I learned with teeth-gnashing envy that my Instonian rivals were to have a shared set in Botany Bay. My father, who had rooms throughout his time at college, finally in the much-prized Rubrics, tried using influence with his former fellow student, the long-serving Junior Dean R.B. McDowell. Nothing doing: there simply was not a room to be had. I went the rounds of student digs and located one in Rathmines, which seemed less bad than the others. I was in the Accommodation Office in Trinity to let them know where I would be staying—all Junior Freshmen had to register their living quarters and flats were not permitted—when Mrs Crawford, the dragon lady in charge, said casually that she thought she might have something for me. A vacancy had come up and I was to have a room in no. 30 in the vast, late nineteenth-century Graduates Memorial Building.

My 'rooms', as they were always grandly termed, consisted of a bedsit with a tiny kitchen off the entrance passageway and a lavatory at the end of the corridor. But they got my life as a Junior Fresh off to a flying start. 'Would you like to come up to my ... ahem ... rooms for a coffee?' I could say to the group of amazing English girls I met on my first day in lectures. It wasn't quite a red two-seater but it would do as a start. Soon I had a positive coterie of friends who dropped by at any time of day: the kettle was almost never off the boil. Having started with very pure principles of nothing but the best freshly ground Bewley's coffee, made in my smart Denby-ware pot, I soon descended to spooning Nescafé out of the jar to make supplementary cups for the latest arrivals. One friend made the rooms a positive home from home whether I was in or out. Ejected sharply from his digs at 8.30a.m. by his Clontarf landlady, he would arrive in no. 30 and install his long frame in the armchair with his feet on the mantel above the gas-fire. I might saunter out to the occasional lecture—they never started before ten o'clock in those pleasantly civilized times—and come back to find my friend in what seemed to be an unchanged position. Whatever he gained from the rapt contemplation of my mantelpiece, it appeared to have served him in good stead as he went on to become the most spectacularly successful member of our student group in the very competitive field of publishing. It's not what you learn at college that matters, it is the mental discipline that you gain while there....

I have never felt in such proud possession of my world before or since as in my first term in rooms in no. 30. Getting up in the morning, I would don my white towelling dressing gown and walk down the flights of stairs from my first floor rooms and out to the bathhouse just across the way. The bathhouse had been endowed by the Earl of Iveagh as a generous gift to the college in 1923. Though the bathhouse is long gone, the plaque with the Latin inscription commemorating the donation by the *Comes de Iveagh* still remains lurking in the Senior Common Room Gents. My father told a follow-up story to that donation. It seems that the College Board of the time thought it would demoralize the young gentlemen to have unlimited free baths, and so decided to impose a sixpenny charge for each bath taken. When the benefactor got to hear of this, he was furious. He provided a further substantial sum of money, enough to ensure that at least a generation of students should not go unwashed for want of a sixpence, and he told the Board that they would regret their parsimony. And so it proved. For, after his death, it appeared that a codicil to his original will revoked a bequest of a million pounds to the College. Whether historically true or simply part of the student folklore of my father's time, it certainly corresponds to the spirit of uptight Protestant penny-pinching and fiscal rectitude which is a part of the Trinity tradition.

I hardly thought of any of that history as I lay, floated—practically swam—in the longest bathtub, with the fastest, gushingest supply of hot water I had ever enjoyed. This was luxury, this was life. And then I could get back into my slippers and dressing-gown and pad over to the little Co-op student shop at the other side of Botany Bay to buy milk and eggs for my breakfast. It is true that after an unfortunate incident one of those mornings when an unwrapped egg cracked in transit, the white towelling dressing-gown carried a yellow stain at its pocket, but that too was merely an honourable badge of service. Back in my rooms I fried my eggs and bacon, toasted my toast, sipped my coffee from my blue Denby-ware mug (no Nescafé for me still at that stage), and felt that God was in Heaven, all was right with the world.

In classes too it was glad, confident morning. Tutorials with R.B.D. French in his rooms in the Rubrics had a comfortably literary feeling to them. We sat around on armchairs and sofas while one or other of the group read out an essay. My first day there, I glanced at an embroidered cushion-cover: 'A Friend in Need', it read in beautifully picked out Gothic lettering. I was imagining R.B.D.'s spinster sister out in Kilternan painstakingly sewing it for him when I read the remainder '... is a Pest'. Perhaps I hadn't got this man exactly right. This, after all, it turned out, was the person who for years wrote the very witty and often devastatingly satiric revues for the student drama society Dublin University Players. He did, though, have his limits. We were studying the Romantic poets, and I (fired up with zeal at my first encounter with Blake) proposed writing an essay on the Prophetic Books. 'Do you need to take us into all that sort of mystery, dear boy?', he replied, with a puff on his pipe. 'Couldn't you do something on the "Songs of Innocence and Experience"?'

I was starting Anglo-Saxon, with all the perverse enthusiasm of someone who positively enjoyed paradigms, and I was also starting Russian. Pete Alscher had studied Russian in Trinity as a subsidiary subject to his Philosophy and, though by my time the College had given up the principle of requiring such a subsidiary—last vestige of an older principle of broad curriculum education—you could still opt to take one on a voluntary basis. So this is what I did with Russian, grandly imagining myself reading *War and Peace* end to end in the original. It didn't work out that way, of course, and a whole shelf of Russian books (including, most accusingly, a twelve-volume complete Tolstoy) now sits gathering dust unopened and unreadable in my study. But there was a thrill in learning the Cyrillic alphabet for the first time, in learning Russian with a heavy Scottish accent from Miss Winifred McBride, in taking conversation classes from Count Tolstoy, who was happy to supply all the conversation himself principally on the subject of his ancestors, among whom Leo the writer, coming from a cadet branch of the family, was mentioned only in passing.

The other part of my life was less exhilarating after a time. I dutifully drove down to Clash each weekend, inspected and counted my sheep that had been looked after by Tom through the week, gave them their autumn dipping to guard against the mange, just as the spring/summer dipping protected them from the fly. But as the days got shorter and the nights got colder through October and November, it seemed less fun to spend from Friday night to Sunday night in an old and damp farmhouse huddled by a Fireside paraffin heater. The scratching sound in the roofboards of the high-ceilinged kitchen began to sound much too loud and strong for mere mice: were those rats above my head? My limited repertoire of cooking learned from Rufus, spaghetti bolognese followed by chilli con carne followed by spaghetti bolognese, began to feel a touch monotonous. (I had made one disastrous attempt to cook a leg of lamb when a friend visited from Belfast, but in spite of my assurances that in France they ate lamb dripping with blood like that, he was unconvinced, and the gory remains stayed with me for weeks after.) Tom's always heartening company and a sense of duty to him and the sheep kept me returning to Clash regularly, but it was less than fun.

Back in College, food was not a problem. It was an obligation of the time for anyone in rooms to eat Commons, the substantial daily meal served in the huge dining hall, with vast canvasses of eighteenth-century worthies looking down on you. At least you had to pay for four such dinners a week at the by no means negligible cost of six shillings a time, so you couldn't afford to waste all that money. The result was that there were two sittings a night at 6.15 and at 7.00 when two hundred young men sat down to a heavy three-course meal of soup, meat and two veg, and pudding to follow, as well as the free glass of porter. I was always considered a desirable dinner companion because of being prepared to pass my porter on to a thirstier neighbour. Women, of course, at this stage, being excluded from rooms, were not among those present. ('Why did we put up with it?' a student contemporary asked me in amazement at a thirty-year reunion; 'why didn't we women revolt, protest, chain ourselves to the railings?' They did by the end of the 1960s, but still in 1965 it just seemed part of an unthinkingly accepted order of things.)

As the Michaelmas Term came to an end, there was the excitement of a first flight to America to look forward to. Pete and Rufus were getting married in New York at Christmas and we were all to come together at the Alschers' apartment on Riverside Drive, my mother from Davis, Rufus and Pete from St Louis and I from Dublin. (Though Rufus would no doubt have been glad for her father to be present at her wedding also, there was no question of our parents being there together: they never were to meet again.) What seemed even more important to me at the time was that I had been cast to play Dan Burke in a Players production of *The Shadow of the Glen* and such is the myopic sense of eighteen-year-old student priorities, I persuaded my mother to change the dates of my flights so I could be back for the start of rehearsals in the New Year. I still had a US passport at the time, so no visas were necessary, but I had to prepare myself with smallpox and other vaccinations, the record of which was stamped into an official booklet guaranteeing that I was free from yellow fever, diphtheria, cholera or the like. So armed, I boarded the Aer Lingus plane at Dublin Airport, still then known as Collinstown. These were still the days of unlimited free drink on airplanes and I made free with it. Here I was 30,000 feet up on a jet travelling to New York, about to land in America: imagine.

Landing in JFK was very definitely coming down to earth. I queued apprehensively with the other Irish travellers to go through Health and Security. A hatchet-faced official looked doubtfully at my official booklet certifying my vaccinations, my freedom from yellow fever and the rest. He then looked up at my long-haired student self and said accusingly: 'Where you been for the last three months?'

'Ireland, please, sir', I stammered, imagining he was suspecting me of having been in some other cholera-ridden country.

'Don't they have any barbers there?'

By the time I passed on to the still longer Immigration queue, I was thoroughly unnerved. I didn't think I was up to the ordeal of strange, forbidding America. I wanted to go back to Ireland, to my rooms in no. 30, to my sheep in Clash where I was safe and not liable to this alienating process of interrogation. My hand trembled as I passed over my blue American passport to the official behind the glass, still more awesome than his colleague in Health and Security. He said not a word but began to check my passport against the listing in a huge volume of undesirables. I knew I would be there: I was about to be deported, I would be put in prison and the key thrown away, I would never get back to Clash again. Finally, he handed back my passport and said unsmilingly: 'Welcome home.'

Acknowledgments

The book's epigraph is taken from 'The Hippopotamus' from *At the Drop of a Hat* by Flanders & Swann © 1957, and appears by permission of the Estates of Michael Flanders & Donald Swann. Administrator Leon Berger: leonberger@donaldswann.co.uk.

Ballinatone church and school (page 31) © Jonathan Billinger.
Old water tower at Negba (page 144) © Bukvoed. These works are licensed under the Creative Commons Attribution-Share Alike 2.0 Generic Licence. To view a copy of this licence, visit http://creativecommons.org/licenses/by-sa/2.0/ or send a letter to Creative Commons, 171 Second Street, Suite 300, San Francisco, California, 94105, USA

Trinity College, Dublin (page 158) with kind permission of Phil Wilson

Border-Leicester sheep (page 165) with kind premission of Jim Redmond, Alexander College, Dublin

Two extracts from this book were first published in the *Dublin Review*; I am very grateful to the editor Brendan Barrington for his sharp-eyed and highly intelligent editing. Eleanor Grene (who suggested the title), Ruth Grene and Bridget Somekh all read drafts of the book and I greatly benefited from their comments, criticism and encouragement in revising it. Jonathan Williams not only acted as my agent but helped me enormously by his patient and precise reading of the text. I am grateful to Andrew and Jane Russell of Somerville Press for their faith in the book and their willingness to publish it, and to Jane Stark for her excellent work on its design.

The book is dedicated to the memory of my parents, those two extraordinary people who shaped the childhood here narrated; no one who knew them can ever forget them.

12/14